SOFTWARE MAINTENANCE MANAGEMENT

A Study of the Maintenance of Computer Application Software in 487 Data Processing Organizations

Bennet P. Lientz
Graduate School of Management, UCLA

E. Burton Swanson
Graduate School of Management, UCLA

ADDISON-WESLEY PUBLISHING COMPANY
Reading, Massachusetts • Menlo Park, California
London • Amsterdam • Don Mills, Ontario • Sydney

Reproduced by Addison-Wesley from camera-ready copy supplied by the author.

Library of Congress Cataloging in Publication Data

Lientz, Bennet P
    Software maintenance management.

    Bibliography: p.
    Includes index.
    1. Computer programming management. I. Swanson,
E. Burton, joint author. II. Title.
QA76.6.L52   001.64'2   80-12154
ISBN 0-201-04205-3

ISBN 0-201-04205-3
ABCDEFGHIJ-AL-89876543210

PREFACE

Maintenance of application software has been often treated as a neglected stepchild to new system development. The former is the product of past romances; new systems represent current hopes and dreams. Understandably, the world of new systems beckons most strongly. However, there may be some limits to current inconstancies. In a recent assessment of software management problems in the Department of Defense, de Roze and Nyman (1978) write:

> The distribution of software costs for all military systems for a given fiscal year shows that 68 percent of known costs are consumed in development of new systems (R&D), while the remaining 32 percent of the known cost is categorized as operation and maintenance (O&M) of systems already in the field. The majority of complex software systems are new and still in the development cycle. As these new systems are deployed, this cost distribution will reverse to emphasize the increased O&M burden. This, coupled with greater system longevity, may

> ultimately result in a five or ten to one ratio of
> O&M cost to R&D cost when viewed over the total
> life cycle of a typical system. With these
> projections, we will need an army of software
> maintainers. (p. 310)

Is maintenance the world of the future? Or is this world, indeed, already here?

This book reports the results of the most extensive public study of maintenance and enhancement of existing application software to date. As such, the objective has been to contribute to an understanding of the maintenance process, to identify and assess key issues, and to suggest future directions for management and research. The emphasis is exploratory, rather than definitive.

The book is intended for use by both researchers and practitioners in the software management field. Researchers should find ample material to motivate their investigations. Practitioners will find a thorough description of the maintenance situations and efforts of a wide distribution of data processing organizations, which should serve as a useful basis of comparison for the practitioners' own organizations. Guidance in approaching the book from either perspective is provided in Chapter 1, the Introduction.

Acknowledgments

The research reported in this book was partially supported by the Information Systems Program, Office of Naval Research, under Contract N00014-75-C-0266, Project Number NR 049-345. Assistance in the administration of the survey was provided by the Education Foundation of the Data Processing Management Association. The support provided by Dr. Roland Spaniol, Director of the Foundation , is gratefully acknowledged, in particular. Some previous work related to software maintenance was also partially supported by the Office of Naval Research.

Los Angeles, California   B.P.L.

February 1980   E.B.S.

CONTENTS

CHAPTER ONE Introduction

This book presents the results of a study of computer application software maintenance in 487 data processing organizations. These applications are mostly of the business type.

Much has been written about the life cycle of computer application software. Within this context, attention has traditionally been focused on the design and development of new software. The maintenance and enhancement of existing software has received relatively little attention. However, there is increasing recognition that maintenance constitutes a persistent and significant burden. The purpose of the study reported here is to contribute to an understanding of maintenance in order that it may ultimately be better managed.

This study reports research results. While not a "how-to-do-it" cookbook, it is intended to be be readable and usable by practicing data processing managers and professionals. For this reason, the book has been organized and presented to maximize efficient access to the research findings for those with a minimal level of background and/or interest in research methods.

The book begins, in this Introduction, with a review of the existing literature on application software maintenance, and a delineation of the basic issues which have been variously raised. The results of a preliminary study are also presented.

In Chapter 2, the research methodology is summarized briefly. This consists essentially of the design and administration of a mail questionnaire survey. This chapter provides a background for the results to follow.

In Chapters 3 through 7 the results of the research are presented. In Chapter 3, the data processing organizations responding to the survey are de-scribed and analyzed. In Chapter 4, major application systems being main-tained by these organizations are similarly treated. In Chapter 5, the nature of the maintenance effort on these application systems is presented and discussed. In Chapter 6, the impact of development tools and organizational controls on the maintenance effort is analyzed. Concluding the presentation of research results in Chapter 7, the problems of maintenance are considered.

Each of Chapters 3 through 7 consists of three parts: (i) a "Summary of Findings" section in which the results presented in the chapter are stated in a straightforward and nontechnical fashion; (ii) a "Basic Descriptive Results" section which presents descriptive statistics and frequency distributions associated with the individual variables of interest in the chapter; and (iii) an "Analysis of Relationships" section in which the associations among the variables of interest are statistically analyzed. This three-part structure enables the casual reader to peruse the research results, simply by reading the first section of each of the five chapters.

In the Conclusion in Chapter 8, an assessment is provided of the implica-tions of the research results for data processing management, and for future research.

2

It is suggested that the reader not attempt to read all chapters and sections of the book in sequence. Two reading strategies will be proposed, directed to researcners and practitioners, respectively.

Researchers may wish to begin by reading Chapters 1 and 2 in their entirety, to obtain a perspective of the problems studied and the research methodology employed. The "Summary of Findings" sections of Chapters 3-7 might next be read, followed by Chapter 8 in its entirety. This should give a good overview of the research findings, and the conclusions drawn. The researcher may then explore the remainder of the book, according to inclination.

The practitioner should also begin with the reading of Chapters 1 and 2. Following this, however, a departure in approach is suggested. The practitioner may find the book most helpful if he/she first applies the research questionnaire to his/her own organization, completing the form in Appendix I as did the 487 organizations responding to the survey. This should assist in the interpretation of the research findings, as well as provide a good basis of organizational comparison. The practitioner might next read the "Summary of Findings" and "Basic Descriptive Results" sections of Chapters 3-7, comparing the survey results to his/her own organizational situation during the course of the reading. The technical "Analysis of Relationships" of these chapters should be perused in a directed fashion, according to questions of appropriate inference which arise. Finally, the Conclusions of Chapter 8 might be read and discussed with regard to their implications for the practitioner's organization.

1.1 Literature Review

Basic issues in application software maintenance, as they have been articulated in the literature to date, may be considered in five groups:

(i)   Conceptual Issues

(ii) Scale-of-effort Issues

(iii) Organizational Issues

(iv) Productivity Technique Issues

(v) Problem Area Issues

We will consider each group of issues in turn.*

Conceptual Issues

A fundamental conceptual issue is: What is meant by the term "maintenance"? Ogdin (1972) distinguishes between maintenance and "modification": "Maintenance is the continuing process of keeping the program running, or improving its characteristics.... Program modification has as its objective the adaptation to a changing environment." Riggs (1969) proposes a more inclusive notion of maintenance: "...the activity associated with keeping operational computer systems continuously in tune with the requirements of users, data processing operations, associated clerical functions, and external demands from governmental and other agencies."

Mooney (1975) argues that maintenance includes three categories of activities: repair, revisions, and enhancements. Canning (1972) identifies four causes of maintenance-type change: (i) program will not run; (ii) program runs but produces wrong output; (iii) business environment changes; (iv) enhancements and optimization. Swanson (1976) presents a system for classifying maintenance into three types: (i) corrective--dealing with failures in

* (The discussion is based on Lientz and Swanson (1978).)

processing, performance, or implementation, (ii) adaptive--responding to anticipated change in the data or processing environments; (iii) perfective-- enhancing processing efficiency, performance, or system maintainability.

Boehm (1976) distinguishes between "software update" and "software repair." The former "results in a changed functional specification" and the latter "leaves the functional specification intact." Other conceptual distinctions may be found in Khan (1975) and Yourdon (1975).

More than terminological preference is at stake. For assessing other maintenance issues, it is important that some common understanding is achieved. Further, when users of application software are assured that systems will be maintained, they should know both what they are getting, and what they are not getting. Here again, a common understanding is necessary.

Scale-of-Effort Issues

The importance of maintenance within the system life cycle has been underscored in the literature by claims as to the scale of effort involved. Canning (1972) writes that "most business users of computers recognize that about 50% of their programming expenses go for 'maintaining' programs already in operation." This is a management issue because of the impact on budgets and perceived benefits of effort. Ditri, et al (1971) cite a similar figure to Canning. Riggs (1969) estimates the demand of maintenance on systems and programming resources to be "possibly as high as 40% to 60% for most companies who have had a computer systems effort for a number of years."

Khan (1975) estimates that up to 40% of programming resources are applied to maintenance. A survey of 905 British installations conducted by Hoskyns Systems Research (1973) also arrived at a figure of about 40%. Liu (1976), on the other hand, writes that "many of installations, especially those in business applications, apply at least 70% of the time of their systems analysts and programmers to the maintenance function."

Brooks (1975) states that the maintenance cost of a program may be 40% or more of the cost of development. Boehm (1976), however, believes that "probably about 70% of the overall cost of software is spent in software maintenance." Comparable figures are to be found in Gunderman (1973), Brantley and Osajima (1975), and Elshoff (1976) .

A related issue is whether the current trend is toward an increase in the scale-of-effort associated with maintenance. Boehm (1976) estimates that "about 40% of the overall hardware-software dollar is going into software maintenance today, and this number is likely to grow to about 60% by 1985. It will continue to grow for a long time, as we continue to add to our inventory of code via development at a faster rate than we make code obsolete."

Still another issue is whether older systems tend to require more maintenance, due to gradual deterioration in the quality of the code and increase in system size and complexity through continual repair and update. Ogdin (1972) and Brooks (1975) provide arguments in support of this view.

Organizational Issues

How should maintenance be organized? A major difference exists in approaches to managing maintenance. In some cases maintenance is performed by a separate maintenance organization. In others it is combined with development. Arguments exist in favor of both approaches. These are summarized very effectively by Canning (1972), who concludes that "separate maintenance is probably the better approach of the two, subject to several conditions."

Mooney (1975) reports a 10% reduction in maintenance effort in one organization where the separate maintenance effort approach was adopted together with several new control procedures.

A closely related issue is the staffing of the maintenance activity. How should the experience of the organization be allocated between maintenance and new system development? Brooks (1975) warns here against using maintenance as a training ground for junior programmers. On the other hand, senior personnel may resist maintenance assignments, if recognition and career advancement are associated with new system development. (See Canning (1972) and Khan (1975).)

Other organizational issues involve the adoption of control procedures in maintenance. Various recommendations here are offered by Riggs (1969), Canning (1972), Mooney (1975), and Liu (1976). Lindhorst (1973) advances the idea of "scheduled maintenance," whereby maintenance is not performed continually as requests are received, but rather is batched periodically.

Productivity Technique Issues

The computer literature abounds with new methods for designing, building, and documenting new software systems. Generally, these methods are intended to increase the overall productivity of the systems and programming staff. To what extent have such productivity techniques been adopted? Where adopted, has system maintainability been enhanced?

Canning (1972) suggests standard data definitions, standard programming languages, a standard set of configuration resources, modular and generalized design, the use of decision tables, installation documentation standards, an on-line change and debugging facility, and automatic test data generators as techniques to be considered for adoption.

Few systematic studies of the benefits in maintenance of various development techniques have been reported. An exception is the Hoskyns survey (1973), where 89% of the users of modular programming reported improved maintainability of their programs.

Problem Area Issues

A final set of issues deals with data processing management's perception of the important problems in maintenance. What problems predominate, and what do these indicate for management? What remedies may be suggested?

Punter (1975) argues that responsibility for maintenance tends to be avoided, inasmuch as maintenance is typically seen as a "necessary evil." Canning (1972) reports that turnover of maintenance personnel may be a serious problem. On the other hand, he asserts that maintenance-type work can actually contribute to higher programmer morale, if the proper people are assigned to it. Riggs (1969) agrees. Canning suggests further that "main tenance" might be renamed "production programming," a term which he finds more professionally appealing.

Mooney (1975) also emphasizes the necessity for the motivation of maintenance personnel. He mentions too the problems of inadequate documentation and too-hasty corrections. Liu (1976) agrees, describing documentation as a "critical issue of system maintenance."

Planning for maintenance is cited as a major problem by Lindhorst (1973).

Missing in the literature are systematic studies of these and other problem area issues. It is thus unknown whether the above viewpoints are representative of data processing management.

1.2 A Preliminary Study

From the literature, it is seen that a variety of issues exist in the maintenance of computer application software. To study these and other issues, the authors have been engaged during the past three years in a long-term research project.

The first phase of the research project involved a pilot survey of 120 data processing organizations, 69 of which completed a questionnaire, describing the characteristics of their maintenance of computer application software. Design and administration of this preliminary study were undertaken in cooperation with Dr. Gerry Tompkins, then a Ph.D. candidate in Computers and Information Systems at the Graduate School of Management at UCLA.

Principal among the findings of the preliminary study were:

(i) Maintenance and enhancement of existing application software consumed an average of 48% of annual systems and programming personnel hours.

(ii) Approximately 60% of the average effort in maintenance and enhancement was devoted to perfective maintenance, i.e., to providing user enhancements, improved documentation, and more efficiently coded programs. Further, within the perfective maintenance category, providing user enhancements accounted for about two-thirds of the average effort.

(iii) Problems of a managerial nature in maintenance and enhancement were seen as more important, on the average, than those of a technical nature. In particular, the problem of user demands for enhancements and exten-sions was regarded as the most important individual problem area.

9

(iv)   Maintenance and enhancement tend to be viewed by management as at least somewhat more important than new system development.

A more detailed discussion of the findings is presented in Lientz, et al (1978). See also the dissertation by Tompkins (1977).

Results of the preliminary study provided the impetus for continuance of the research in the form of a follow-up survey of more concentrated depth and expanded coverage. In the chapter to follow, the design and administration of this survey is described.

CHAPTER
TWO Survey Design
and Administration

Based upon the results of the preliminary survey discussed in the previous chapter, plans for a more extensive questionnaire survey were set. The objectives of this more extensive survey were to validate and extend the findings of the first survey.

An important aspect of the survey plan involved the choice of the population to be surveyed. In this regard, the Data Processing Management Association (DPMA) was contacted with respect to making available a mailing list of those of its members who were managers of data processing organizations. From this contact there evolved a more extensive cooperation by the Education Foundation of the DPMA in the administration of the survey. Mr. Roland Spaniol, Director of the Education Foundation, was instrumental in arranging this cooperation. Provided for the survey by DPMA were: (i) mailing labels for a randomly-selected sample of 2,000 of its members in the

United States and Canada who were employed as a Director/Manager/Supervisor of Data Processing; and (ii) a cover letter supporting the research purposes of the questionnaire.

The DPMA was judged to be the ideal organization for a membership survey, given its substantial size (22,302 members as of December 31, 1975), diverse organizational and geographical representation, and professional commitment to data processing management.

The decision to sample, rather than survey all of the nearly 7,000 DPMA members who are Directors/Managers/Supervisors of Data Processing was made on the basis of cost-effectiveness. The sample size of 2,000 was judged to be of probable sufficiency for ultimate analytic purposes, given an estimate of the likely response rate to be in the range of 10% to 40%, with 20% seen as "most likely." Random selection of the sample was of course vital to ensure representativeness.

The second important aspect of the survey design was the development of the questionnaire. Based upon the results of the preliminary survey discussed earlier, the questionnaire employed was modified and consolidated iteratively. Inasmuch as the new survey was to be conducted by mail, special attention was given to reduction of the questionnaire length, so as not to discourage the prospective respondent. The final version of the questionnaire consisted of nineteen pages, nevertheless.

A copy of the final version of the questionnaire is included in Appendix I, together with a copy of the DPMA cover letter which accompanied it. In the Introduction to the questionnaire (included on page 2), it is requested that the questionnaire be completed "by the manager of the Data Processing Department, with the assistance of his or her staff." This request was made because several of the questionnaire items called specifically for the judgment of the manager, while others called specifically for matters of fact within the department.

One further important feature of the questionnaire should be noted in its Introduction. It was recognized that some of the facts called for might not easily be obtainable, given the data maintained by the organizations surveyed. Questionnaire items seeking these facts were thus accompanied with the following check-box:

Check the applicable statement:
The above answer is:
Reasonably accurate, based on good data_____
A rough estimate, based on minimal data_____
A best guess, not based on any data_____

This permitted the respondents to estimate and guess, where good data was not available, and encouraged a more complete filling-in of the questionnaire. In addition, the questionnaire data was substantially enriched for analysis.

Administration of the questionnaire was undertaken in the Fall, 1977. A total of 1979 questionnaires were distributed by bulk mail. (Of the 2,000 pre-addressed labels, 21 were judged not usable for various reasons.) A cover letter and postage-prepaid return envelope were included with each questionnaire distributed. After approximately three weeks, a reminder postcard was sent, in addition.

The total number of completed responses to the questionnaire was 487, a response rate of 24.6%. This was somewhat in excess of what had been expected. Comments on the questionnaires indicated further that the questions were answered by most respondents with considerable thought and diligence.

Four questionnaires were returned incomplete for various reasons, by means of the return envelopes provided. Three questionnaries were returned without the original envelopes having been opened. Two questionnaires were returned completed, but too late to be included in the analysis.

Data from the completed questionnaires was keypunched into cards, five cards to a questionnaire, and verified. The data was then loaded as an SPSS

(Statistical Package for the Social Sciences) file for analysis. Validating of the data was performed by computational procedures, making use of various "rea sonableness checks" wherever possible. For a detailed description of SPSS, see Nie, et al, 1975. This reference should also be useful for reviewing definitions of some of the statistical terms used in the chapters to follow.

In Chapters 3 through 7 to follow, the findings of the questionnaire survey are presented. This presentation follows roughly the order in which the data were statistically analyzed. A discussion of the approach to this analysis appears in Appendix II. Basic descriptive results appear according to the key:

Subject	Items	Chapter
The DP Organizations	1.1-1.7	3
The Application Systems	2.1-2.10	4
The Maintenance Effort	2.11-2.14	5
The Impact of Development Tools and Operational Controls	2.15	6
The Problems of Maintenance	2.16	7

Analysis of the relationships among the data represented by the questionnaire items is cumulative. Thus, in Chapter 3, the relationships among the data describing the data processing organizations are analyzed. In Chapter 4, the relationships among the data describing the application systems are analyzed, and these data are related to the data describing the data processing organizations. In Chapter 5, the relationships among the data describing the maintenance processes are analyzed, and these data are related further to both the application system data and the data processing organization data. The overall sequence of analysis follows from the presumption that the data processing organizations established the contexts for the application systems, which, in turn, provide the contexts for the maintenance undertaken.

CHAPTER
THREE The Data
Processing
Organizations

In this chapter, a description and analysis of the data processing organizations responding to the survey is presented. This description and analysis is based upon Part I of the questionnaire, which consists of seven items, 1.1 through 1.7. (See Appendix I.)

3.1 Summary of Findings

Maintenance consumes about half the time of the systems and programming staff of the average data processing department. Managers indicated this was true two years ago, as well as today, and there is thus no acknowledged trend toward an increase in the relative effort on maintenance.

However, larger data processing organizations tend to spend greater proportions of their time on maintenance. This is true whether the size of the organization is measured in terms of annual equipment budget, or in terms of total staffing levels. Thus, as a data processing organization grows, it can expect to spend proportionally more time on maintenance.

The relative time spent on maintenance also is found to vary significantly by industry, though this may be due largely to the differences between industries in the sizes of the data processing departments.

Most interestingly, departments where maintenance is organized separately from new system development tend to spend _less_ relative time on maintenance. Since the motivation to establish a separate maintenance unit would presumably be based on the need to cope with a significant effort in maintenance, this finding is perhaps an indication that separate organization of maintenance leads to increased efficiency in its performance. This conclusion is further strengthened, when it is considered that a separate maintenance organization exists more frequently among the larger data processing departments, which tend to spend relatively larger amounts of time on maintenance.

Only 16.2% of the data processing departments surveyed organized maintenance separately from new system development.

In terms of their own time, more than two-thirds of the department managers surveyed tend to give equal, if not more, time to new system development. However, the greater the proportion of staff time spent on maintenance, and the greater the increase of this proportion over the last two years, the more of the manager's own time is similarly spent on maintenance.

More than half of the data processing managers surveyed felt their departments were "somewhat understaffed." This tendency to feel understaffed increased somewhat as the size of the annual equipment budget increased, up to the $500,000 to $1,000,000 range. The perceived adequacy of staffing also varied significantly by industry, with government and education constituting two examples of industries where management felt more understaffed than the average across all industries.

3.2 Basic Descriptive Results

Item 1.1 of the questionnaire asks that the respondents indicate the industry to which the organization served by the data processing department belongs. The breakdown of the results is shown in Figure 3.1. It is seen that representation from a wide cross section of industries is included.

The industry categories used in Item 1.1 are those employed by the DPMA in recording its own membership. It is thus possible to verify that responses to the survey were representative. The six industry categories most represented among survey respondents, in decreasing order, are:

1. Other non-manufacturing (1)
2. Insurance (5)
3. Government (4)
4. Primary/fabricated metal (3)
5. Banking/credit agency (6)
6. Other manufacturing (2)

The numbers in parentheses indicate the corresponding rank ordering of these categories among all 22 categories for the membership as a whole, for individuals who are a Director/Manager/Supervisor of Data Processing. It is seen that the six most predominate categories are identical, though not exactly in the same order, indicating that the sample closely resembles the population.

Within the industry category of other non-manufacturing, two important additional categories were identified among those written in by respondents: health (frequency: 13, 2.7%) and wholesale/retail (frequency: 29, 6.0%). These were then split out as separate from miscellaneous for subsequent analysis.

17

Questionnaire Item 1.2 groups the data processing organizations according to the size of their data processing budgets. The results are shown in Figure 3.2. As expected, the smaller organizations exceed the larger in number. However, an excellent representation across budget level categories is achieved.

Item 1.3 asked respondents to indicate staffing levels of the data processing departments. As shown in Figures 3.3 and 3.4, the results indicate a roughly exponential distribution of both total number of personnel and number of programmer/analysts, with a decreasing number in each successive frequency category. Also characteristic is a small number of extremely large organizations; sixteen organizations reported a total staffing level of 241 persons or more, and nine organizations reported a number of programmer/ analysts of 121 or more. Because of the characteristics of these distributions, the natural logarithm transformations of both the total number of data processing personnel and the number of programmer/analysts are used in the analysis of relationships with other variables, where a normal distribution is assumed (see Section 3.3 to follow).

In Questionnaire Item 1.4, respondents were asked whether in their departments applications programmers and/or system analysts responsible for the maintenance of existing application systems are organized separately from those responsible for new system development. A total of 79 (16.2%) indicated that maintenance is organized separately. A majority, 408 (83.8%), indicated that maintenance is combined with new system development.

Item 1.5 sought to probe the extent to which maintenance tends to dominate the systems and programming time of the organizations surveyed. The results are shown in Figure 3.5, and are in part somewhat unexpected. Maintenance is seen to consume about half the time of systems and programming staff, on the average. However, over a two year interval, there is no reported increase in this percentage despite reports in the literature that it has been growing. If anything, a small decline in the relative maintenance effort may have taken place. However, these percentages are not weighted according to absolute size of the maintenance efforts. (In Section 3.3 to follow, further analysis of this result is presented.)

In the case of Item 1.5, respondents were also asked to indicate the quality of data upon which their answers were based. Results are shown in Figure 3.6. It is seen that only about half of the organizations possess good data on the percent of staff time currently allocated to maintenance.

Questionnaire Item 1.6 sought the judgment of the manager of data processing as to the relative demands of maintenance on his or her own time. The results, shown in Figure 3.7, are again somewhat surprising. Despite previous research evidence that management tends, on the average, to view maintenance as "somewhat more important" than new system development (see Section 1.2), here it is found that, in terms of their own time, 71.7% of the managers give equal, if not more, time to new system development.

Questionnaire Item 1.7 completes Part I of the questionnaire. Managers were asked in this item to evalute the sufficiency of current staffing levels. Results are shown in Figure 3.8, and are not particularly surprising. As might be expected, the most frequent response was "somewhat understaffed."

Figure 3.1

To what industry does the organization served by the Data Processing Department belong?

		Absolute Frequency	(Percent)
Manufacturing industries:			
a.	Data Processing Equipment 4 (0.8)		
b.	Instruments/Electrical	10	(2.1)
c.	Chemical/Allied Products 13 (2.7)		
d.	Printing/Publishing	12	(2.5)
e.	Food/Tobacco	21	(4.3)
f.	Primary/Fabricated Metal	40	(8.2)
g.	Transportation Equipment 12 (2.5)		
h.	Petroleum/Coal/Rubber	19	(3.9)
i.	Paper/Paper Products	18	(3.7)
j.	Textiles/Apparel	7	(1.4)
k.	Other	34	(7.0)
Non-manufacturing industries:			
l.	Insurance	49	(10.1)
m.	Banking /Credit Agency	38	(7.8)
n.	EDP Services	19	(3.9)
o.	Education	32	(6.6)
p.	Government	48	(9.9)
q.	Public Utility	17	(3.5)
r.	Investment	4	(0.8)
s.	Mining/Construction	8	(1.6)
t.	Transportation	15	(3.1)
u.	Consultants	4	(0.8)
v.	Other	61	(12.5)
	Valid Response Total	485	(99.6)

Figure 3.2

What is the annual budget of the Data Processing Department for data processing equipment rental, maintenance, and amoritzation expense?

		Absolute Frequency	(Percent)
a.	$4,000,000 or more	35	(7.2)
b.	Less than $4,000,000 but $2,000,000 or more	27	(5.5)
c.	Less than $2,000,000 but $1,000,000 or more	52	(10.7)
d.	Less than $1,000,000 but $500,000 or more	72	(14.8)
e.	Less than $500,000 but $250,000 or more	71	(14.6)
f.	Less than $250,000 but $125,000 or more	81	(16.6)
g.	Less than $125,000	141	(29.0)
	Valid Response Total	479	(98.4)

Figure 3.3

What is the total number of equivalent full-time personnel in the Data Processing Department?

Mean Number: 45.4

Median: 17.2

Number	Absolute Frequency	(Percent)
1–10	174	(35.7)
11–20	94	(19.3)
21–30	57	(11.7)
31–40	23	(4.7)
41–50	32	(6.6)
51–60	13	(2.7)
61–70	11	(2.3)
71–80	10	(2.1)
81–90	6	(1.2)
91–100	6	(1.2)
101–	58	(11.7)
Total Valid Response	484	(98.4)

Figure 3.4

Of the total number of equivalent full-time data processing personnel, how many work as applications programmers and/or systems analysts?

Mean Number: 17.2 (37.9%)

Median: 4.9 (28.5%)

Number	Absolute Frequency	(Percent)
1-5	244	(50.1)
6-10	81	(16.6)
11-15	39	(8.0)
16-20	26	(5.3)
21-25	17	(3.5)
26-30	11	(2.3)
31-35	6	(1.2)
36-40	6	(1.2)
41-45	3	(0.6)
46-50	4	(0.8)
51-	42	(8.4)
Total Valid Response	479	(98.4)

Figure 3.5

In terms of the total person-hours worked annually by applications programming and systems analysis personnel, what percentage is currently spent in each of the following activities:

	Mean	SD
Application system maintenance:	48.8	22.3
New application system development:	43.3	21.1
Other:	7.9	13.0
Total:	100.0	

Two years ago, what were the percentages?

	Mean	SD
Application system maintenance:	50.8	26.3
New application system development:	41.9	24.9
Other:	7.3	13.7
Total:	100.0	

Figure 3.6

Estimated Quality of Data by Respondents

	Answer Based On Good Data	Answer Based On Minimal Data	Answer Not Based On Any Data	No Indication
Percent effort in maintenance, current:	52.0%	34.9%	11.7%	1.4%
Percent effort in maintenance, two years ago:	36.1%	39.4%	20.3%	4.1%

Figure 3.7

As the manager of the Data Processing Department, how demanding on your own time are the problems which arise in application system maintenance, when compared to those which arise in new application system development?

		Absolute Frequency	(Percent)
a.	New System development problems by far the more demanding	92	(18.9)
b.	New system development problems somewhat more demanding	130	(26.7)
c.	Maintenance and new system development problems equally demanding	127	(26.1)
d.	Maintenance problems somewhat more demanding	97	(19.9)
e.	Maintenance problems by far the more demanding	38	(7.8)
Valid Response Total:		484	(99.4)

Figure 3.8

Relative to the tasks at hand, how would you evaluate the current level of staffing of the Data Processing Department on the whole?

		Absolute Frequency	(Percent)
a.	Substantially understaffed	56	(11.5)
b.	Somewhat understaffed	256	(52.6)
c.	Neither understaffed nor overstaffed	161	(33.1)
d.	Somewhat overstaffed	14	(2.9)
e.	Substantially overstaffed	0	(0.0)
	Valid Response Total	487	(100.0)

3.3 Analysis of Relationships

In this section, the relationships among the variables represented by questionnaire Items 1.1 through 1.7 (Part I) are analyzed.

Of particular interest is the variable, percent time currently been spent on maintenance (see Item 1.5), and its possible variation according to type and size of the data processing organization. A reasonable conjecture is that larger, more mature organizations represent larger accumulations of applications, and, hence, must spend relatively more time on maintenance. Limited support for this conjecture was obtained from the survey results. An analysis of variance of percent time currently being spent on maintenance according to size of the data processing equipment budget was performed. The variance was found to be significant at the weak level of $s = 0.105$, and linearity was found to be significant at the $s = 0.008$ level. Larger data processing equipment budgets are thus associated with larger relative efforts in maintenance. However, the differences are not, on the average, dramatic. The range of the mean percent time on maintenance across all budget categories extended only from 44.4% to 53.5%. Thus, even the largest of data processing organizations manage to strike a balance between maintenance and new system development, on the average.

Further support for the hypothesis that larger organizations spend more relative time on maintenance was provided by several correlation coefficients computed. Percent time currently being spent on maintenance correlated significantly and positively with the natural log transformations of both the total number of data processing personnel ($r = 0.209$, $s = 0.001$) and the number of programmer/analysts ($r = 0.177$, $s = 0.001$). Thus, an increase in the staff of a data processing organization is likely to reflect the growing relative demands of maintenance.

Percent time in maintenance was also found to vary significantly, at the $s = 0.005$ level, according to industry served, as shown in Figure 3.9. An interpretation here is that maturity in data processing applications varies by

28

Figure 3.9

Variation in Percent Time in Maintenance by Industry

Industry	Mean	Standard Deviation	Sample Size
EDP Services	65.26	17.83	(19)
DP Equipment Manufacturing	60.00	29.72	(4)
Investment	56.25	18.87	(4)
Banking Credit	55.66	24.05	(38)
Insurance	55.18	20.20	(49)
Health	52.69	27.81	(13)
Education	50.53	22.62	(32)
Government	50.42	20.00	(48)
Transportation	50.33	21.25	(15)
Other Manufacturing	49.97	24.06	(34)
Public Utility	48.41	19.39	(17)
Food/Tobacco	46.86	22.40	(21)
Construction/Mining	45.63	26.92	(8)
Electrical Instruments	45.50	18.92	(10)
Petroleum/Coal/Rubber	45.00	20.95	(19)
Paper	44.78	21.43	(18)
Wholesale/Retail	43.72	23.02	(29)
Transportation Equipment	43.33	24.98	(12)
Primary Fabricated Metal	42.88	20.52	(40)
Other Non Manufacturing	41.42	21.96	(19)
Printing/Publishing	39.58	15.32	(12)
Chemical/Allied	39.38	20.49	(13)
Textiles Apparel	28.57	25.28	(7)
Consulting	26.25	17.02	(4)
Total Sample:	48.60	22.29	(485)

industry. Where applications are extensive, e.g., in banking and insurance, relatively more time is spent on maintenance. This interpretation received some support from a cross-tabular analysis of the variance of data processing equipment budgets across industries. A chi-square analysis revealed this variance to be significant at the $s = 0.065$ level, with both the banking/credit and insurance industries, for example, tending to have larger installations than the average across all industries. Other explanations of the variance in percent time in maintenance by industry may, of course, also be possible.

Also of interest was the variance of percent time currently spent on maintenance according to the organization of maintenance, i.e., whether maintenance is organized separately from new system development (see Item 1.4). As was noted in Chapter 1, advocates for the separate organization of maintenance have argued that it can contribute to a more efficient effort in maintenance. Significant support for this claim was obtained from the present survey. Variance in percent of time spent on maintenance was significant at the $s = 0.024$ level, with a mean of 43.3% for an organization with a separate maintenance unit, and a mean of 49.5% for those without such a unit.

It is also reasonable to suppose that a separate maintenance unit would tend to be adopted in larger, more mature data processing organizations, with larger maintenance needs. (If this were the case, it would lend further strength to the above finding that organizations with separate maintenance units spend relatively less time in maintenance.) However, a contingency table analysis of the organization of maintenance according to data processing equipment budget gave mixed results. The chi-square statistic was not significant. On the other hand, Kendall's Tau, which takes into account the ordinal nature of the equipment budget classification, was significant at the $s = 0.045$ level, and the relative increase in the use of a separate maintenance unit for larger budgeted organizations was thus confirmed. On the whole, then, larger organizations appear able to use separate maintenance units to achieve efficiency in maintenance through specialization.

As was discussed in the previous section (see Figure 3.5, page 24), the mean percent time currently spent on maintenance, for all responding organizations, is 48.8%, which may be compared to the mean of 50.8% claimed for two years ago.   Applying the Student's t-test, the hypothesis that these percentages are significantly different was rejected at the s = 0.035 level. Thus, it cannot be concluded that the percent time spent on maintenance has changed on the whole over the two year period.   Again, this result contradicts the claims in the literature that the relative effort in maintenance is growing rapidly.

Management's perception of the adequacy of staffing levels (Item 1.7) was also analyzed in terms of its relationships to other Part I variables.   In a cross-tabular analysis with data processing equipment budget levels, perceived adequacy of staffing was found to vary significantly (the chi-square statistic was significant at the s = 0.088 level, and Kendall's Tau was significant at the s = 0.042 level).   Interestingly, it was found that as the size of the annual equipment budget increased, up to the $500,000 to $1,000,000 budget range, there was an increased expression of being understaffed.   To illustrate, for the smallest budgets (less than $125,000), 44.0% of the respondents felt correctly staffed and 53.9% felt understaffed; for budgets in the $500,000 to $1,000,000 range, only 20.8% felt correctly staffed, and 76.4% felt understaffed. However, for still larger budgets, the increase in feeling understaffed did not persist.   Any interpretation here is tenuous, but one possibility may be that as the data processing organization goes through its basic growth stage (see Nolan, 1973), the feeling of being understaffed is characteristic, as user demands for new applications predominate.

Perceived adequacy of staffing was also cross-tabulated according to industry.   A chi-square analysis indicated a significant relationship at the s= 0.063 level.   Industries feeling more understaffed than average included government (50.0% somewhat understaffed, 20.8% substantially understaffed) and education (37.5% somewhat understaffed, 21.9% substantially under-staffed.   These may be contrasted with the primary fabricated metal industry, for example (27.5% somewhat understaffed, 17.5% substantially understaffed).

Another cross-tabular analysis revealed no relationship between perceived adequacy of staffing and the organization of maintenance.   Apparently, the organization of maintenance into separate units, which has been seen to be associated with reduced relative time spent on maintenance, does not translate significantly into a feeling of being more correctly staffed, on the whole.

Similarly, an analysis of variance of percent time currently spent on maintenance with perceived adequacy of staffing disclosed no significant relationship. However, statistical significance apart, the mean percent time on maintenance was successively larger as staffing was perceived to be the more inadequate. This result is consistent with previous research findings that management, faced with a budget cut, would cut back more from new system development than from maintenance. (See Lientz, et al, 1978.)

Finally, the demands of maintenance on the data processing manager's own time (see Item 1.6) were analyzed with respect to other variables in Part I of the questionnaire. One finding, which was not surprising, was that the variance of percent staff time currently spent on maintenance was significant with respect to the demands of maintenance on the manager's time. A significance level of less than $s = 0.001$ was found in the analysis of variance performed, and linearity was similarly significant at the less than $s = 0.001$ level. Clearly where more staff time is devoted to maintenance, more management time must also be spent. A closely related finding was that the change in percent staff time spent on maintenance over the last two years was also related to the demands of maintenance on a manager's own time (variance was significant at the $s = 0.066$ level, and linearity was significant at the $s = 0.021$ level.) The greater the increase in percent staff time spent on maintenance during the last two years, the greater the current demands of maintenance on the manager's own time.

A cross-tabulation of the demands of maintenance on the data processing manager's own time by industry and by size of the equipment budget showed no relationships. A cross-tabulation by the organization of maintenance produced a significant chi-square statistic, but linearity was not significant, and the result was judged uninterpretable. The same was the case when a cross-tabulation by perceived adequacy of staffing was attempted.

CHAPTER
FOUR The Application
Systems

In the previous chapter, we considered the responses to Part I of the survey questionnaire. In Part I, the questionnaire items dealt with the data processing department as a whole. In this chapter and those to follow, the responses to Part II of the questionnaire are considered. In Part II, the respondents are asked to report on an individual application system which meets three criteria: (i) has been operational one year or longer; (ii) represents a significant investment of departmental time and effort; (iii) is considered by management to be of fundamental importance to the organization (see Appendix I). Here we consider the application systems reported, as they were described in Items 2.1 through 2.10 of the questionnaire. In the next chapters (5-7), the maintenance conducted on these same systems is treated.

Following the format of the previous chapter, we summarize first the findings. Basic descriptive results and an analysis of relationships follow successively.

4.1 Summary of Findings

Applications - type, size, age

The applications described were extremely diverse in nature; however, the classical application types were heavily represented. (A breakdown of applications is given in Figure 4.1.) Payroll was the most frequently described application, numbering 50, about 10% of the total. Order entry, billing and invoicing, inventory control, general ledger, and accounts receivable were the other applications most frequently described. Diversity was represented by 75 systems classified as "other," of which no two were alike.

The median age of the application systems reported was 3 years 4 months. The mean age was higher (4 years 9 months) due to the presence of a few very old systems (20 over 12 years old). (See Figure 4.2.)

The average application system consisted of approximately 55 programs, 23,000 source statements, 6 master files, 13 megabytes in data base, and 26 pre-defined user reports (based on computed medians in each category). Generally the data typifies a substantial data processing application. However, the variance in application system size was large, and the distribution was exponential in form, including a large number of very small systems, and a small number of extremely large systems.

The various measures of application system size were significantly inter-correlated, as would be expected. About 50% of the variance in the number of programs in the application systems was explained by the number of pre-defined user reports included, suggesting a possible useful predictive relationship.

The annual reported growth rate of the size of an application system averaged roughly 10% (measured in terms of number of programs, number of source statements, and number of pre-defined user reports). The average annual growth rate of the data base was less, about 5%. On the whole, these growths reflect increased organizational uses of the application systems maintained.

Older systems tended to be larger in size than younger systems, and evidence, both direct and indirect, indicated that this was due to the continued growth with age of operational systems. Older systems tended also to have slower growth rates than younger systems, and the growth curves of application systems thus appear to follow a classical growth curve pattern, where limited resources are involved. (In Chapter 8, it will be suggested that the particular curve which applies is the logistic curve.)

The number of source statements per program tended to be slightly larger, the older the system, lending some support to those who argue that programs grow in complexity as they are maintained. (See, for example, Brooks, 1975). As we will see this has substantial impact on managerial and technical practice.

More than half of the application systems were written principally in COBOL (52%), and almost another quarter were written principally in RPG (22%). This is representative of mixes of languages commonly cited, for traditional data processing applications.

The use of the RPG programming language was associated with the younger and smaller systems being maintained. The use of FORTRAN, though infrequent, was associated with older, smaller systems. PL/1 was associated with larger systems. COBOL was representative of the average age and size.

Data base management systems tended to be associated with the younger and larger application systems being maintained, as would be expected.

A relatively small number of the application systems (70, less than 15%) made use of a data base management system.

Tools and Techniques

The relative frequencies with which certain productivity tools, methods, and techniques were used in the development of the application systems described were also computed. Most frequently used were the chief programmer team (38%), decision tables (34%), and structured programming (30%). Less frequently used were the structured walk-through (17%), test data generators (16%), data base dictionary (15%), HIPO (7%), and automated flow-charting (5%).

Of the development tools, methods, and techniques, HIPO was significantly associated with younger systems. The use of automated flowcharting was significantly associated with older systems. Data base dictionaries and test data generators were significantly associated with larger systems. No other relationships between the use of tools, and system age and size were established at the conventional significance levels. On the whole, this is somewhat surprising. To advocates of productivity aids, it may also be disappointing, in that no clear trend toward increased use of these tools emerges. However, this does not negate the possibility of productivity gains achievable through use of the tools.

Interestingly, larger growth rates in the number of application system programs were found to be significantly associated with the use of a data base management system and a data base dictionary. Because these tools are also associated with larger systems which tend on the whole to grow more slowly, this suggests that growth is facilitated by their use. A possible interpretation is that the effective management of the data base resource, through the use of these tools, permits more extended applications. Note, however, that the maintenance burden may thereby increase.

Application system age was also found related to two of the organizational variables described in Chapter 3. Older systems were found significantly related to larger data processing equipment budgets and to a greater percent of total staff time devoted to maintenance. This is seen as consistent with the view that larger budgets represent gradual accumulations of applications over time.

Application programming language use was similarly related to the data processing equipment budget. RPG is used almost exclusively in the smallest budget categories, and PL/1 tends toward use only in the larger. COBOL completely dominates all other languages, except in the smallest and largest of installations.

Of the development tools, methods, and techniques, four tended to be associated with larger equipment budgets: data base dictionary, test data generators, HIPO, and chief programmer team. This is not surprising, since larger budgets may more easily absorb the overhead involved in the use of the tools. Productivity gains may thus be achieved with this larger base.

4.2 Basic Descriptive Results

Item 2.1 of the questionnaire requested that the application system selected be identified and described. Except for portions of the questionnaire set aside for remarks, this item was the only open-ended question included. The resulting application descriptions were, as might be expected, various. However, an attempt was made to classify them by organizational function. The results are shown in Figure 4.1. As expected, the classical data processing applications, e.g., payroll, order entry, billing and invoicing, are most heavily represented. Included in the category "other" are all those applications, a total of 75, which resisted classification into groups of two or more.

It must be emphasized that the classification categories for Item 2.1 are not mutually exclusive. For example, "billing and invoicing" overlaps as a category with "accounts receivable," and, in a different way, with "patient billing." For this reason, some care must be taken in interpretation.

Item 2.2 requested that respondents indicate the date (month and year) on which the application system became operational. From this, the current age of each application system, in number of months, was computed. The resulting distribution is shown in Figure 4.2. The mean age was found to be 56.6 months, and the standard deviation, 44.1 months. While the most frequently reported ages are in the one to three year range, a few very old systems, twenty over twelve years old, are included.

It is noted from Figure 4.2 that 28 systems are reported to be of age 12 months or less, of which 10 are of age 6 months or less. It was decided not to exclude these systems from further analysis, although they do not all meet the stated criterion of being operational one year or longer.

The use of data base management systems software is currently of wide interest in management applications. In questionnaire Item 2.3, it was asked whether a data base management system was employed in the processing of

Figure 4.1

Application Systems

Classification of Functions:

Function	Absolute Frequency	(Percent)
Other	75	(15.4)
Payroll	50	(10.3)
Order Entry	36	(7.4)
Billing and Invoicing	34	(7.0)
Inventory Control	25	(5.1)
Accounts Receivable	21	(4.3)
General Ledger	21	(4.3)
Insurance Policy Processing	18	(3.7)
Sales Analysis	14	(2.9)
Demand Deposits	13	(2.7)
Student Registration	12	(2.5)
General Accounting	11	(2.3)
Loan Processing	10	(2.1)
Financial Management	9	(1.8)
Bill of Materials	8	(1.6)
Life Insurance	8	(1.6)
Production Information	8	(1.6)
Materials Requirements	8	(1.6)
Customer Information	7	(1.4)
Accounts Payable	6	(1.2)
Labor Hour Distribution	6	(1.2)
Materials Management	6	(1.2)
Utility Billing	6	(1.2)
Unspecified	6	(1.2)
Auto Insurance	5	(1.0)

Figure 4.1 (Continued)

Function	Absolute Frequency	(Percent)
Budget Accounting	5	(1.0)
Claims Administration	5	(1.0)
Product Costing	5	(1.0)
Management Reporting	4	(0.8)
Patient Billing	4	(0.8)
Payment Settlement	4	(0.8)
Agent System	3	(0.6)
Distribution Management	3	(0.6)
Property Tax	3	(0.6)
Service Management	3	(0.6)
None	3	(0.6)
Advertising Information	2	(0.4)
Course Scheduling	2	(0.4)
Freight Dispatching	2	(0.4)
Law Enforcement	2	(0.4)
Personnel	2	(0.4)
Property Management	2	(0.4)
Retirement System	2	(0.4)
Shop Floor Control	2	(0.4)
Trust Accounting	2	(0.4)
Vehicle Maintenance	2	(0.4)
Vehicle Registration	2	(0.4)
Total	487	(100.0)

Figure 4.2

On what date (month and year) did the application system become operational?

System Age* (Number of Months)	Absolute Frequency	(Percent)
1 - 6	10	(2.1)
7 - 12	18	(3.7)
13 - 18	49	(10.1)
19 - 24	40	(8.2)
25 - 30	54	(11.1)
31 - 36	41	(8.4)
37 - 42	34	(7.0)
43 - 48	16	(3.3)
49 - 54	27	(5.5)
55 - 60	20	(4.1)
61 - 66	20	(4.1)
67 - 72	10	(2.1)
73 - 78	13	(2.7)
79 - 84	11	(2.3)
85 - 90	21	(4.3)
91 - 96	16	(3.3)
97 - 102	9	(1.8)
103 - 108	7	(1.4)
109 - 114	12	(2.5)
115 - 120	7	(1.4)
121 - 126	8	(1.6)
127 - 132	0	(0.0)
133 - 138	3	(0.6)
139 - 144	1	(0.2)
145 -	20	(4.1)
Total Valid Responses	467	(95.9)

* as of December, 1977

the application system. A total of 70 systems (14.4%) were reported as using a data base management system; 417 (85.6%) were reported as making no such use. This result was not unexpected, considering the range of age of the application systems. As can be seen, the time needed for technological change to fully penetrate information system applications is often substantial.

Questionnaire Items 2.4 through 2.9 dealt principally with various measures of the size of the application system: number of programs; number of source statements; number of data files; number of data base bytes; and number of pre-defined user reports. Using the median number reported in each category, the average application system described was of the following size:

54.6	Programs
23,000	Program source statements
6.1	Data files
13.3	Data base (megabytes)
26.1	Pre-defined user reports

However, the variance in each category was large, and the average was thus representative of relatively few systems.

In Figures 4.3 through 4.7 on the following pages, the distributions associated with the above measures of size are described more fully. Note that in each case, the variation in size approximates an exponential distribution, with a decreasing number of occurrences in each category, and with a significant number of occurrences of exceptionally large sizes. For this reason, the mean of each distribution is about twice the value of the median. Because of the nature of these distributions, a natural logarithm transformation of each will be used in analyses of the sections to follow, where a normal distribution is to be assumed.

Figure 4.3a

What is the total number of programs <u>currently</u> included in the application system maintenance? (The term "program" is associated here with a block of source language statements compiled or assembled as a unit.)

Mean Number: 126.6

Median: 54.6

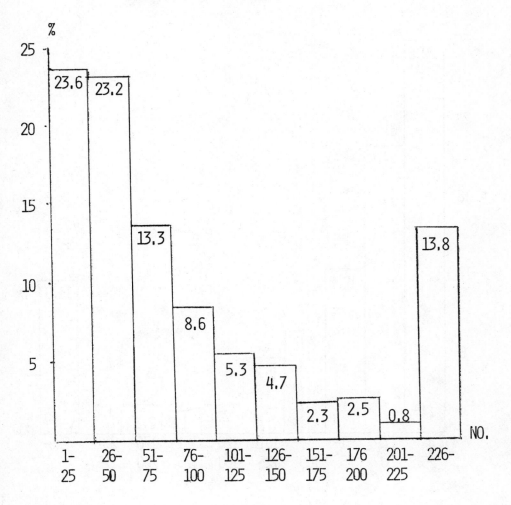

TOTAL VALID RESPONSES: 479

Figure 4.3b

What was the total number of programs included in the application system <u>one</u> <u>year ago</u>?

Mean Number: 115.6
Median: 46.4

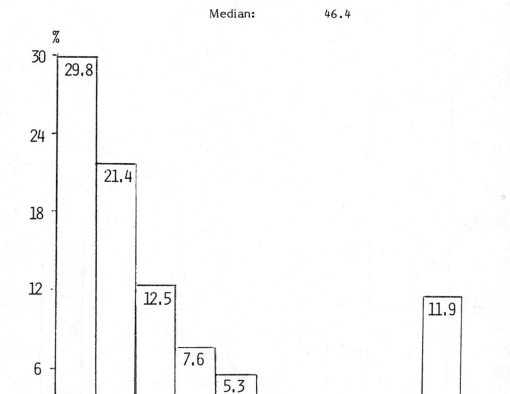

TOTAL VALID RESPONSES: 467

Figure 4.4a

What is the total number of source language statements (excluding comments) currently included in the application system maintained?

Mean Number (Thousands): 48.0

Median: 23.0

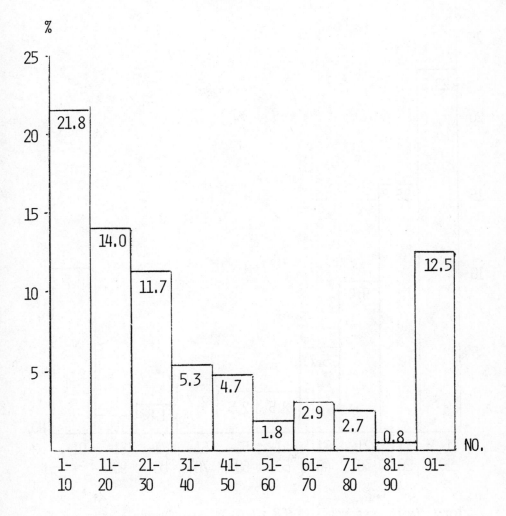

TOTAL VALID RESPONSES: 381

Figure 4.4b

What was the total number of source language statements (excluding comments) included in the application system <u>one year ago</u>?

Mean Number (Thousands): 43.6
Median: 19.5

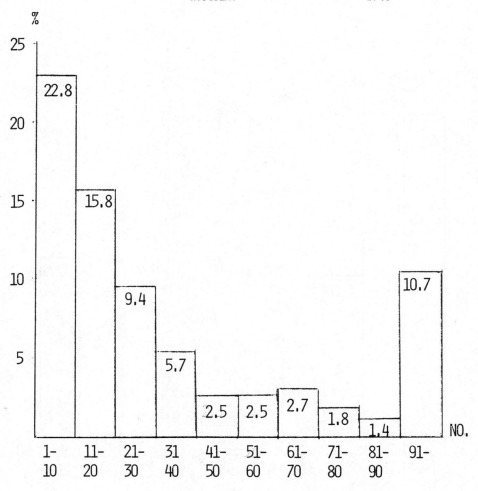

TOTAL VALID RESPONSES: 368

46

Figure 4.4c

Of the total number of source language statements currently maintained, what percentage is written in each of the following languages?

Language	Mean Percent	Principal Language Percent*
COBOL	51.6	52.0
Assembler	11.9	10.5
PL/1	3.2	3.5
RPG	22.4	21.8
FORTRAN	2.4	0.2
Others	7.7	6.0

*The principal language of an application system is defined as the language in which more than half of the total number of source statements is written.

NOTE TO PUBLISHER: SHOW AS TWO PIE CHARTS

Figure 4.5

How many individual data files currently make up the data base associated with the application system? (The term "data base" is defined here simply as the set of master files associated with the system.)

Mean Number: 16.0
Median: 6.1

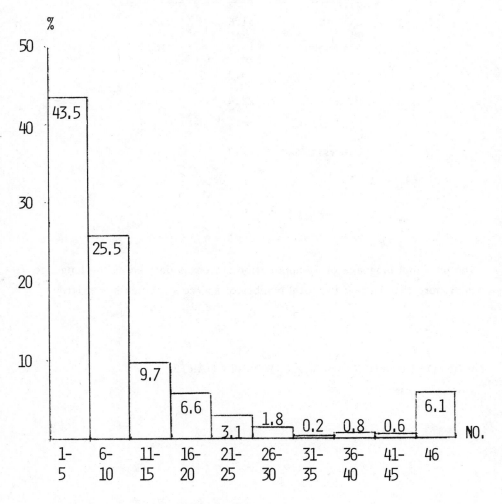

TOTAL VALID RESPONSES: 477

Figure 4.6a

What is the <u>current</u> size of the data base, measured in total number of bytes (or the equivalent)?

Mean Number (Millions):   43.8
Median: 13.3

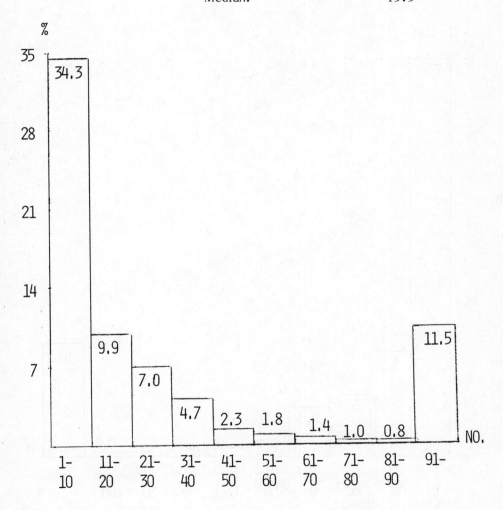

TOTAL VALID RESPONSES: 365

Figure 4.6b

What was the size of the data base, measured in total number of bytes (or the equivalent) <u>one year ago</u>?

Mean Number (Millions):	41.6
Median:	11.9

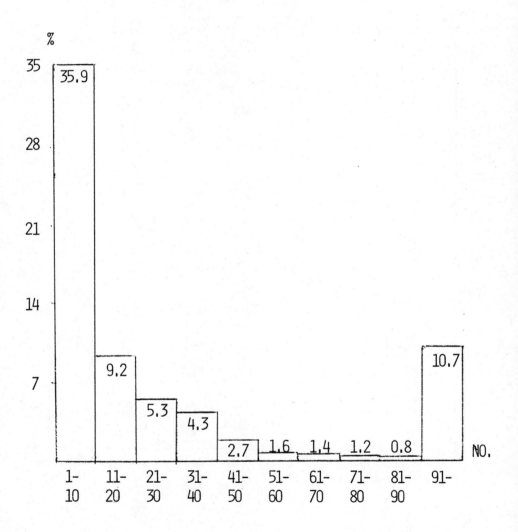

TOTAL VALID RESPONSES: 358

Figure 4.7a

How many pre-defined user reports are <u>currently</u> associated with the application system maintained?

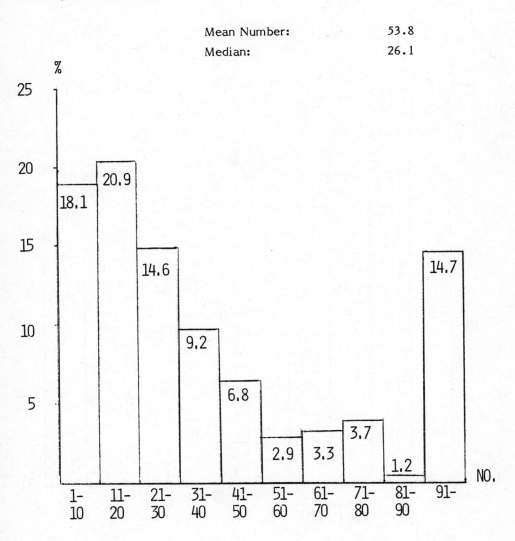

Mean Number: 53.8
Median: 26.1

TOTAL VALID RESPONSES: 465

51

Figure 4.7b

How many pre-defined user reports were associated with the application system <u>one year ago</u>?

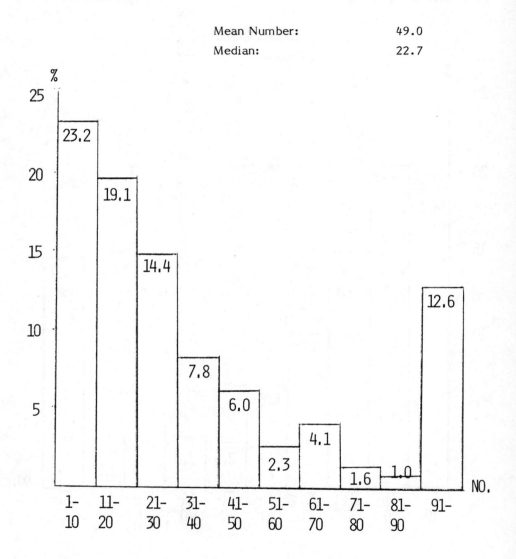

Mean Number: 49.0
Median: 22.7

TOTAL VALID RESPONSES: 450

In the case of the measures of application size (number of programs, number of program source statements, number of data base bytes, and number of pre-defined user reports) respondents were asked to indicate both current numbers and numbers for one year ago. The purpose was to obtain some indication of the growth rates of application systems. Using the mean numbers associated with each measure, the average system may be seen to have grown at the following annual rates:

Number of programs:	9.5%
Number of program source statements:	10.1%
Number of data base bytes:	5.3%
Number of pre-defined user reports:	9.8%

Respondents were also asked (in Item 2.6) to indicate the percentage distribution of program source statements in terms of programming languages. Mean percents reported are shown in Figure 4.4c. As expected, COBOL dominates. However, the figures may be somewhat misleading, since they do not reflect the absolute numbers of source statements reported. As an example, since RPG is more typical of smaller systems, the percentage probably exaggerates its representation among all source statements maintained.

Figure 4.4c also reports the frequency with which each language represents the principal language of the application systems described. The principal language is defined as the language in which more than half of the total number of system source statements is written. As is seen, the principal language percentages correspond closely to the mean percentages.

Also of interest is the extent to which management possesses good data on application system size. In responding to questionnaire Items 2.4

through 2.9, it was in most cases requested that the basis for data for each answer be indicated (see the questionnaire, Appendix I). Results are shown in Figure 4.8. It is seen that most organizations possessed good data on current number of programs and programming languages used; about half possessed good data on current data base size and number of pre-defined user reports; relatively few possessed good data on current number of source statements. Further, when numbers are sought for one year ago, the availability of good data drops substantially in each case, giving some indication of the extent to which adequate historical records are not maintained. The implications of these findings for the management of maintenance will be discussed further in Chapters 5 and 6.

Finally, in questionnaire Item 2.10, it was requested that the use of various tools and techniques in the development of the application system be indicated. The results are shown in Figure 4.9. Somewhat surprising is the wide acceptance reported of the chief programmer team concept. However, this may be more apparent than real, since, in our judgment, respondents tended to give the term a very wide interpretation.

On the whole, the use of development tools, methods, and techniques is not particularly widespread. It must be borne in mind, however, that these figures pertain to operational systems of average age exceeding three years. The figures for systems currently under development might conceivably differ.

Figure 4.8

Management Data on Application System Size

	Answer Based On Good Data	Answer Based On Minimal Data	Answer Not Based On Any Data	No Indication
Number of programs, current:	82.1%	14.2%	1.8%	1.8%
Number of programs, one year ago:	68.0%	22.2%	5.3%	4.5%
Number of program source statements, current:	32.4%	31.8%	23.6%	12.1%
Number of program source statements, one year ago:	20.1%	33.7%	30.0%	16.2%
Number of source statements, language distribution:	84.6%	11.7%	2.1%	1.6%
Number of data base bytes, current:	50.7%	30.2%	9.2%	9.9%
Number of data base bytes, one year ago:	37.6%	32.6%	15.6%	14.2%
Number of pre-defined user reports, current:	56.5%	26.1%	10.1%	7.4%
Number of pre-defined user reports, one year ago:	48.5%	28.7%	12.3%	10.5%

Figure 4.9

Which of the following tools, methods, and techniques were employed in the development of the applicaton system maintained?

		Absolute Frequency	(Percent)
a.	Decision tables	164	(33.7)
b.	Data base dictionary	73	(15.0)
c.	Test data generators	80	(16.4)
d.	Structured programming	145	(29.8)
e.	Automated flowcharting	24	(4.9)
f.	HIPO (Hierarchy plus Input-Process-Output) Design Aid Technique	34	(7.0)
g.	Structured walk-through	82	(16.8)
h.	Chief programmer team	187	(38.4)
	Others	47	(9.6)

NOTE TO PUBLISHER: SHOW AS 2 BAR CHARTS BY FREQUENCY AND PERCEN

Figure 4.10

Correlation Coefficients Between Measures
of Application System Size*

	Number of Programs	Number of Source Statements	Number of Data Files	Number of Data Base Bytes	Number of Pre-Defined User Reports
Number of Programs		.644 (415) s=.001	.329 (473) s=.001	.326 (409) s=.001	.707 (462) s=.001
Number of Source Stamtements			.231 (411) s=.001	.407 (369) s=.001	.613 (404) s=.001
Number of Data Files				.216 (410) s=.001	.277 (460) s=.001
Number of Data Base Bytes					.277 (403) s=.001
Number of Pre-defined User Reports					

* First-order Pearson correlation coefficients, using natural logarithm transformations of measures of system size. Numbers in parentheses indicate
number of cases in computation.

4.3 Analysis of Relationships

Of principal interest in this secton is the analysis of application system size and growth.

The various measures of application system size: number of programs, number of source statements, number of data files, number of data base bytes, and number of pre-defined user reports, were found to be significantly intercorrelated, as shown in Figure 4.10.   All first-order correlation coefficients are seen to be significant at the s = 0.001 level. Particularly interesting is the strength of the relationship between number of programs and number of pre-defined user reports (r = 0.717), which suggests that the latter might be a significant factor in the explanation and prediction of the former.

Note that in computing the above correlation coefficients, natural loga-rithm transformations of the basic size measures were used, to achieve consistency with the necessary normality assumptions. In the subsequent dis-cussion of this section, wherever these size measures are involved, it should be understood that these same transformations were also used.

Each of the measures of system size was correlated with current system age (compiled from Questionnaire Item 2.2). Four of the five measures cor-related significantly and positively: number of pre-defined user reports (r = .171, s = 0.001); number of source statements (r = .156, s = 0.001); number of data base bytes (r = .139, s = 0.003); and number of programs (r = .118, s = 0.005).   Thus, older systems tend to be larger systems. Two possible explanations may be suggested: first, that systems developed more recently tend to be smaller than those developed earlier; second, that systems tend to grow once they become operational. The first explanation seems somewhat unlikely. The second may be explored by means of an analysis of other data gathered.

In the case of the four measures of size which correlate significantly and positively with system age, data was obtained both for current size and for size one year ago (see Questionnaire Items 2.4, 2.5, 2.8 and 2.9). It was thus possible to compare mean current sizes with mean sizes of one year ago, applying Student's t-test to the differences. These differences were established to be significant at the less-than .001 level, confirming the reported growth in each category (see page 58). Thus, the assertion that systems tend to grow once they become operational is supported by both direct and indirect survey results.

Also of interest is an examination of the relationship of the growth rates of application systems to system age. Using the data for current size and size one year ago, growth rates for four measures were computed and correlated to system age: growth in number of programs ($r = -0.243$, $s = 0.001$); growth in number of source statements ($r = -0.189$, $s = 0.001$); growth in number of data base bytes ($r = -0.194$, $s = 0.001$); and growth in number of pre-defined user reports ($r = -0.195$, $s = 0.001$). Thus, while systems tend to grow with age the rate of growth slows correspondingly.

It was asked to what extent the size of the application system might account for the relationship found between growth rates and system age. Partial correlation coefficients for growth rates and system age were thus computed, controlling for the absolute size of the system. In each case, the partial correlation coefficient was found to be larger than the first-order coefficient, and significant at the $s = 0.001$ level. This confirms the importance of system age in accounting for the growth rates of the application systems.

It has been argued in the literature that individual programs tend to grow in size, and become more complex, as they are maintained. The partial correlation coefficient between number of program source statements and system age was thus computed, controlling for number of programs. A significant relationship was found ($r = 0.110$, $s = 0.014$), confirming the contention that individual programs tend to grow in size as they are maintained.

The use of alternative programming languages, development tools and techniques, and data base management systems was also explored, in terms of their relationship to system size, growth, and age.

An analysis of variance of system age according to the use of development tools and techniques and data base management systems produced only limited results of statistical significance. The use of the tool HIPO was significantly associated with younger systems at the s = 0.055 level. The use of automated flowcharting, on the other hand, was found to be associated with older systems, at the weak s = 0.108 significance level. There was some tendency for the use of a data base dictionary, structured programming, and the structured walk-through to be associated with younger systems, but this tendency was not of notable statistical significance. The use of decision tables, test data generators, and the chief programmer team showed no relationship at all to system age. The use of a data base management system was significantly associated with younger systems at the s = 0.047 level.

Variance of system age according to principal programming language used was also found to be significant, at the s = 0.002 level. The use of RPG was associated with younger systems (mean age: 44.3 months), while the use of assemblers was associated with older systems (mean age: 70.6 months). The use of COBOL (mean age: 54.3 months) was representative of the overall average. FORTRAN tended to be used with somewhat older systems (mean age: 60.4 months), in those few cases where it was reported to be the principal language. The variance in the age of the systems using PL/1 was unusually large, and the mean age was judged not meaningful.

An analysis of variance of the number of application system programs according to the use of development tools and techniques and data base management systems was further conducted. Significantly associated with larger numbers of programs were: data base dictionaries (s = 0.091), test data generators (s = 0.058), and data base management systems (s = 0.002).

Also interesting was an analysis of variance of the growth rate of the number of programs according to the use of these same tools and techniques. Significantly associated with larger growth rates were: data base dictionaries (s = 0.008), chief programmer team (s = 0.051), and data base management systems (s = 0.006). The associations for data base dictionaries and data base management systems suggest that these techniques may facilitate a more rapid development and expansion of operational systems than might otherwise be achieved. This interpretation is based upon the more frequent use of these techniques for the development of larger systems, which, on average, have lesser growth rates.

Variance in both the number of application system programs and the total number of source statements was also significant, at $s = 0.001$ levels, according to principal programming language used. PL/1 tended to be associated with larger systems, by both measures. Assembler tended to be associated with somewhat larger systems, again by both measures. The use of COBOL was associated with systems of average size, by both measures. RPG was associated with smaller systems, in terms of number of source statements, and average systems, in terms of number of programs. The use of FORTRAN was associated with small systems, by both measures.

Of potential interest to planners of large scale application systems is the accurate estimation of future amounts of software to be developed and maintained. Such amounts may then be used as a basis for staffing decisions. The feasibility of using statistical methods to assist in software estimation was explored by means of a regression model in which the dependent variable was taken to be the number of programs in the application system, and the independent variables were: system age, number of data base bytes, number of pre-defined user reports, and the use or non-use of a data base management system and various development tools and techniques. As before, natural logarithm transformations of the size variables were employed, to meet normality assumption requirements. Stepwise regression was also used. It was found that about 52% of the variance in the number of programs in application systems was explained by the number of pre-defined user reports involved. Another one to two percent was explained by the size of the data base. But the remaining variables were of negligible value in the estimation model.

The relationship of the application systems described in Part II of the questionnaire to the organizational variables described in Part I was also sought. An analysis of variance of system age by data processing equipment budget was performed, and it was found significant at the $s = 0.007$ level. Older systems were thus found to be associated with larger equipment budgets, a finding consistent with the proposition that such budgets represent gradual accumulations of data processing applications over time. Also consistent with this view was the slight positive relationship found to exist between system age and the percent of staff time devoted to maintenance in the organization ($r = 0.085$, $s = 0.034$).

Of some interest also is the association of principal programming language used with the size of the data processing equipment budget. The results of a cross-tabular analysis are shown in Figure 4.11, and are found to be highly significant. The complete domination of COBOL is striking, in all but the smallest and largest of installations. RPG is associated with a majority of installations in the smallest budget category, and is well represented up to the $500,000 per year level. But its use in larger installations is negligible. In contrast, PL/1 tends to be used only in these same larger installations. The use of assemblers is evenly distributed across all categories. A few FORTRAN systems are represented in the smallest budget category, but the use of FORTRAN otherwise is nil.

Also analyzed was the extent to which use of development tools, methods, and techniques varied according to the size of the data processing equipment budget. It was expected here that certain tools would be used more frequently by the larger data processing organizations, which could more easily absorb the overhead cost involved. In Figure 4.12, a breakdown of the usage of development aids according to annual equipment budget is presented. It is seen that six of the eight aids tend to be used more frequently, the larger the level of the equipment budget. Only decision tables and automated flow-charting are not significantly associated with budget level by either of the two statistical tests employed.

Figure 4.11

Cross-Tabulation of Principal Programming Languages by
Data Processing Equipment Budgets[*]

DP Budget	COBOL	Assembler	PL/1	RPG	FORTRAN	Other	Row Total
Less Than $125th	34	11	1	69	6	16	137
	24.8	8.0	0.7	50.4	4.4	11.7	29.5%
	13.4	21.6	5.9	65.1	75.0	55.2	
	7.3	2.4	0.2	14.9	1.3	3.4	
$125th - 250th	48	8	1	18	1	2	78
	61.5	10.3	1.3	23.1	1.3	2.6	16.8%
	19.0	15.7	5.9	17.0	12.5	6.9	
	10.1	0.9	0.2	3.0	0.0	0.9	
$250th - 500th	47	4	1	14	0	4	70
	67.1	5.7	1.4	20.0	0.0	5.7	15.1%
	18.6	7.8	5.9	13.2	0.0	13.8	
	10.1	0.9	0.2	3.0	0.0	0.9	
$5000th - 1 Mil	50	12	5	1	0	1	69
	72.5	17.4	7.2	1.4	0.0	1.4	14.9%
	19.8	23.5	29.4	0.9	0.0	3.4	
	10.8	2.6	1.1	0.2	0.0	0.2	
$1 - 2 Mil	39	6	4	1	0	0	50
	78.0	12.0	8.0	2.0	0.0	0.0	10.8%
	15.4	11.8	23.5	0.9	0.0	0.0	
	8.4	1.3	0.9	0.2	0.0	0.0	

Figure 4.11 (Continued)

DP Budget	COBOL	Assembler	PL/1	RPG	FORTRAN	Other	Row Total
$2 - 4 Mil	19	5	0	0	0	1	25
	76.0	20.0	0.0	0.0	0.0	4.0	5.4%
	7.5	9.8	0.0	0.0	0.0	3.4	
	4.1	1.1	0.0	0.0	0.0	0.2	
$4 Mil or More	16	5	5	3	1	5	35
	45.7	14.3	14.3	8.6	2.9	14.3	7.5%
	6.3	9.8	29.4	2.8	12.5	17.2	
	3.4	1.1	1.1	0.6	0.2	1.1	
Column Totals	253	51	17	106	8	29	464
	54.5%	11.0%	3/7%	22.8%	1.7%	6.3%	100.0%

Raw Chi Square = 171.59 with 30 degrees of freedom

Significance = less than 0.001

*Key to Table Entries

Example	Interpretation
34	count
24.8	row percentage
13.4	column percentage
7.3	total percentage

Figure 4.12: Continued

Use of Development Productivity Aids	Less Than $125K	$125K-250K	$250K-500K	$500K-1M	$1M-2M	$2M-4M	$4M or More	Totals	Statistical Significance Levels*
HIPO	5 (3.5%)	3 (3.7%)	2 (2.8%)	6 (8.3%)	7 (13.5%)	5 (18.5%)	5 (14.3%)	33 (6.9%)	0.006, 0.000
Structured Walk-Through	21 (14.9%)	10 (12.3%)	12 (16.9%)	13 (18.1%)	10 (19.2%)	8 (29.6%)	7 (20.0%)	81 (16.9%)	‾, 0.049
Chief Programmer Team	36 (25.5%)	32 (39.5%)	30 (42.3%)	31 (43.1%)	30 (57.7%)	10 (37.0%)	12 (34.3%)	181 (37.8%)	0.003, 0.001

* Only significance levels less than 0.100 are shown.
The first level in each pair corresponds to the raw chi square statistic,
the second to Kendell's Tau B.

Figure 4.12: Frequency of Use of Productivity Aids by Data Processing Equipment Budget

Annual Data Processing Equipment Budget

Use of Development Productivity Aids	Less Than $125K	$125K-250K	$250K-500K	$500K-1M	$1M-2M	$2M-4M	$4M or More	Totals	Statistical Significance Levels*
Decision Tables	48 (34.0%)	29 (35.8%)	19 (26.8%)	24 (33.3%)	18 (34.6%)	7 (25.9%)	17 (48.6%)	162 (33.8%)	None
Database Dictionary	19 (13.5%)	5 (6.2%)	13 (18.3%)	8 (11.1%)	10 (19.2%)	7 (25.9%)	9 (25.7%)	71 (14.8%)	0.040, 0.015
Test Data Generators	16 (11.3%)	10 (12.3%)	11 (15.5%)	12 (16.7%)	8 (15.4%)	9 (33.3%)	12 (34.3%)	78 (16.3%)	0.007, 0.001
Structured Programming	40 (28.4%)	22 (27.2%)	15 (21.1%)	25 (34.7%)	21 (40.4%)	9 (33.3%)	13 (37.1%)	145 (30.3%)	0.049
Automated Flowcharting	6 (4.3%)	3 (3.7%)	4 (5.6%)	2 (2.8%)	4 (7.7%)	1 (3.7%)	4 (11.4%)	24 (5.0%)	None

CHAPTER
FIVE The Maintenance
Effort

This chapter continues the analysis of the application systems reported in Part II of the survey questionnaire. Whereas the previous chapter dealt with system characteristics such as application type, age, and size, the present chapter is devoted to a study of the maintenance performed on these same systems as reported in Items 2.11 through 2.14 of the questionnaire. The impact of development tools and organizational controls, and the problems of maintenance are discussed in succeeding chapters.

Following the format of the previous two chapters, the findings will first be summarized. Basic descriptive results and an analysis of relationships follow in that order.

5.1 Summary of Findings

Somewhat more than a third of the application systems described are maintained by a single person. Another third are maintained by two individuals, and somewhat less than a third are maintained by three persons or more. Many of the individuals assigned to maintenance of the systems have other assignments as well. Thus, when the number of person-hours spent on maintenance of the system is considered, it is found that approximately 3/4 of the systems are maintained by the equivalent of one full-time person or less. Further, substantially more than half of the systems are maintained by the equivalent of half a full-time person or less.

The allocation of maintenance time to various task types was also assessed. Corrective maintenance, i.e., emergency program fixes and routine debugging, accounted for slightly more than 20% of the total, on the average. Adaptive maintenance, i.e., the accommodation of changes to data inputs and files, and to hardware and system software, accounted for slightly less than 25%. Perfective maintenance, i.e., enhancements for users, improvement of program documentation, and recoding for efficiency in computation, accounted for over 50%. In particular, enhancements for users accounted for 42% of the total maintenance effort, on the average. This result corresponds closely to results reported from an earlier study. (Lientz, et. al., 1978.)

The allocation of time spent in providing user enhancements was itself investigated. Almost 70% of this effort was seen to consist of giving the user "more," i.e., new reports, or additional data in existing reports. About 10% of the effort was directed toward reformatting existing reports, somewhat more than 10% was spent in data condensation and report consolidation, and about 10% was devoted to "other" enhancements. Thus, comparatively little attention is given to "filtration" of data for management.

Of the number of individuals assigned to maintenance of an application system, somewhat less than half also worked on the development of this same system, on the average. This relative fraction, computed for each application system, was termed the "relative development experience" of the maintainers of the system.

The magnitude of a maintenance effort was found to be explained, in part, by the combined effects of four variables: system age, system size, relative amount of routine debugging, and the relative development experience of the maintainers. Five causal paths appeared to relate the complex of variables.

The first path indicates that with increased system age, system size tends to increase, leading to a greater effort in maintenance. The increase in system size may be attributed in large part to the incorporation of user enhancements and extensions.

A second path is a variant of the first. In this, the relative amount of routine debugging mediates between the size of the system and the level of effort in maintenance. Larger systems are seen to require relatively more routine debugging, perhaps because the location and elimination of bugs becomes a more complex task, and the overall effort in maintenance rises in turn, reflecting the need to allocate more time to debugging.

A third causal sequence indicates that with increased system age, the relative development experience of the maintainers tends to decline due to organizational turnover and change, which leads in turn to an increased effort in maintenance, perhaps because of a decline in maintenance productivity.

The fourth causal path is a variant of the third. In this, the relative amount of routine debugging mediates between the relative development experience of the maintainers and the level of effort in maintenance. A decline in relative development experience leads to an increase in the relative amount of routine debugging performed, probably because lack of familiarity with the design necessitates more time being spent to find and eliminate bugs, which results in turn in an increase in the overall level of the maintenance effort.

The final causal path indicates that increased system age leads directly to an increase in the level of effort in maintaining the system. This relationship, which was found to be rather weak, may, perhaps, be explained by the tendency of a system to become less well-ordered as it ages, and thus harder to maintain, regardless of size, or the skills of the maintainers.

In summary an analysis of relationships among several variables indicates that five causal paths exist, each of which supports the proposition that an increase in the age of a system tends to lead to an increase in the level of effort in maintenance.

Suggestions on how to manage the level of effort in maintenance are given in Chapter 8.

5.2 Basic Descriptive Results

Item 2.11 of the questionnaire requested that respondents indicate the total number of person-hours expended annually on maintenance of the application system described. The results are shown in Figure 5.1. If 2,000 person-hours is accepted as roughly equivalent to one person-year, it is interesting to note that approximately three-quarters of the application systems are maintained by the equivalent of one person or less. Even more striking, substantially more than half of the systems require the equivalent of half a person or less.

Item 2.12 requested that respondents indicate the allocation of the total maintenance time reported according to various problem areas. The results are shown in Figure 5.2, and correspond closely to results of the pilot survey reported previously (summarized in Section 1.2 of this monograph).

From the results of the pilot survey, it was expected that enhancements for users would account for a significant percentage of time spent in maintenance. Questionnaire Item 2.13 was thus formulated to explore user enhancements in more depth. In particular, it was desired to assess whether user enhancements consisted primarily in giving the user "more," as opposed to improving the quality of what was already received. The results are shown in Figure 5.3. The extent to which giving the user "more" dominates is striking, consisting of close to 70% of the enhancements effort, compared to 10% spent in reformatting, somewhat more than 10% in condensation and consolidation, and about 10% in "other." Thus, although experts have long called for more emphasis on "filtration" in providing information for users (e.g., see Ackoff, 1967), giving the user "more" remains the dominant mode of response.

Questionnaire Item 2.14 consisted of two parts. Respondents were asked first to indicate the total number of individuals currently assigned to maintenance of the application system. This gave a second measure of the demands of maintenance of the system on the organization's resources, apart from the total number of person-hours involved (see Item 2.11). Respondents were then asked to indicate the number of those assigned who had worked previously on the development of the application system. This gave some

Figure 5.1

What is the total number of person-hours now expended annually on maintenance of the application system?

	Mean Number:	2768
	Median:	827

Number			Absolute Frequency	(Percent)
1	–	1000	277	(56.9)
1001	–	2000	63	(12.9)
2001	–	3000	30	(6.2)
3001	–	4000	18	(3.7)
4001	–	5000	14	(2.9)
5001	–	6000	15	(3.1)
6001	–	7000	7	(1.4)
7001	–	8000	8	(1.6)
8001	–	9000	3	(0.6)
9001	–		22	(4.4)
Total Valid Responses:			457	(93.8)

Figure 5.2

Of the total number of person-hours now expended annually on maintenance of the application system, what percentage is expended in each of the following problem areas:

		Mean Percent
a.	Emergency program fixes	12.4
b.	Routine debugging	9.3
c.	Accommodation of changes to data inputs and files	17.4
d.	Accommodation of changes to hardware and system software	6.2
e.	Enhancements for users	41.8
f.	Improvement of program documentation	5.5
g.	Recoding for efficiency in computation	4.0
	Others	3.4
	Total:	100.0

Figure 5.3

Of the total number of person-hours now expended annually on providing enhancements for users in maintenance of the application system, what percentage is expended in each of the following problem areas:

		Mean Percent
a.	Providing new, additional reports	40.8
b.	Adding data to existing reports	27.1
c.	Reformatting existing reports, without changing their data content	10.0
d.	Condensation of data in existing reports	5.6
e.	Consolidation of existing reports, reducing the number of reports	6.4
	Others	10.1
	Total:	100.0

indication of the extent to which systems tend to be maintained by the same individuals who develop them. Results are shown in Figures 5.4a and b. Note that somewhat more than a third of the systems are maintained by a single individual, another third by two individuals, and somewhat less than a third by three or more. Almost a third of the systems are maintained by individual(s) with no experience in their prior development.

Finally, in the cases of questionnaire items 2.11, 2.12, and 2.13, it was requested that management indicate the quality of the data possessed on the effort in system maintenance. Results are shown in Figure 5.5. It is seen that less than 40% of the organizations surveyed possess good on the total number of annual person-hours allocated to maintenance of the system described.

Figure 5.4a

What is the total number of individuals currently assigned (in whole or in part) to maintenance of the application system?

	Mean Number:	2.6
	Median:	1.4

Number	Absolute Frequency	(Percent)
1	169	(34.7)
2	158	(32.4)
3	63	(12.9)
4	19	(3.9)
5	19	(3.9)
6	4	(0.8)
7	8	(1.6)
8	7	(1.4)
9	3	(0.6)
10 or more	17	(3.4)
Total Valid Responses	467	(95.9)

Figure 5.4b

Of the total number of individuals currently assigned, how many worked previously on the development of this same application system?

Mean Number: 1.2

Median: 0.4

Number	Absolute Frequency	(Percent)
0	150	(30.8)
1	200	(41.1)
2	72	(14.8)
3	18	(3.7)
4	12	(2.5)
5	2	(0.4)
6	2	(0.4)
7	2	(0.4)
8	3	(0.6)
9	0	(0.0)
10 or more	6	(1.2)
Total Valid Responses	467	(95.9)

Figure 5.5

Management Data on System Maintenance Effort

	Answer Based On Good Data	Answer Based On Minimal Data	Answer Not Based On Any Data	No Indication
Number of annual person-hours:	36.1%	40.5%	17.2%	6.2%
Allocation of annual person-hours:	30.0%	50.9%	16.0%	3.1%
Allocation of annual person-hours in enhancements:	25.7%	45.0%	20.1%	9.2%

5.3 Analysis of Relationships

Of principal interest in this section are relationships which explain the magnitude and allocation of the maintenance effort.

The magnitude of the effort in maintaining the application system described was reflected in the responses to Questionnaire Items 2.11 through 2.14. These responses indicated: (i) the total number of person-hours expended annually on maintenance of the system; (ii) the percentage allocation of maintenance person-hours according to various problem areas; (iii) the percentage allocation of maintenance person-hours spent on providing user enhancements according to various subproblem areas; (iv) the total number of individuals assigned in whole or in part to maintenance of the application system; (v) the total number of individuals assigned to maintenance of the application system who worked previously on the development of the system.

The relative development experience of the maintainers of the application system was computed by dividing the number of maintainers who worked on the development of the system by the total number of maintainers, as indicated in Questionnaire Item 2.14. This computed variable could thus vary between 0 and 1. The mean relative development experience was found equal to 0.481, and the standard deviation, 0.426.

As noted in Section 5.2, the total number of person-hours in system maintenance and the total number of system maintainers were both substantially skewed in distribution. To meet the normality assumptions of parametric analysis, the natural logarithm transformation of each was thus used throughout, and should be so understood in the paragraphs which follow.

A first relationship investigated was that between the magnitude of effort in maintenance, as represented by total number of person-hours and total number of persons assigned, and the allocation of maintenance time between different problem areas. First-order Pearson correlation coefficients were computed. It was found that both larger numbers of person-hours and larger numbers of persons assigned were associated with relatively more time allocated to the task of routine debugging (r = 0.169, s = 0.001; r = 0.132, s = 0.002). Other correlation coefficients were also significant, but less so. Larger numbers of person-hours were associated with less relative time on emergency fixes (r = -0.079, s = 0.046); less relative time on accommodating data and file changes (r = -0.100, s = 0.016); and more relative time on recoding for computational efficiency (r = 0.066, s = 0.081). Larger numbers of persons assigned were associated with less relative time on providing user enhancements (r = -0.067, s = 0.075); and more relative time on recoding for computational efficiency (r = 0.078, s = 0.047). Because none of these less significant correlations is of size $|r| \geqslant 0.100$, further analysis was judged unwarranted. However, it remains to provide an interpretation for the association of the level of effort in maintenance with the allocation of this effort to routine debugging.

The relationship between magnitude of effort in maintenance and the allocation of time spent in providing user enhancements was next investigated. Since there is only the slightest evidence that relative time spent on providing user enhancements itself varies with magnitude of effort, no results of striking significance were expected here. Indeed, little was discovered. Computing first-order Pearson correlation coefficients as before, it was found that greater numbers of maintenance person-hours were associated with relatively less time on reformatting existing reports (r = -0.088, s = 0.030); and that greater numbers of maintenance persons assigned were associated with relatively less time on providing new reports (r = -0.079, s = 0.044), and relatively more time on adding data to existing reports (r = 0.065, s = 0.080). However, none of these correlations were of size $|r| \gtrsim 0.100$, and in the context of all of the coefficients computed, these findings were judged uninterpretable. On the whole, then, the allocation of time in providing user enhancements does not appear to vary substantially with the level of effort in maintenance.

The relationships among the allocations of maintenance time to various problem areas were also investigated. Since these allocations were computationally dependent, in that they had to sum to 100%, a built-in bias toward negative covariance existed. Thus, only positive correlation coefficients were regarded as noteworthy. Two relationships were established: relative time in emergency fixes was positively associated with relative time in routine debugging ($r = 0.076$, $s = 0.047$); and relative time in program documentation was positively associated with relative time in recoding for computational efficiency ($r = 0.123$, $s = 0.003$). The first relationship may indicate that as corrective maintenance varies, it manifests itself in both its "emergency" and "routine" components. The second relationship may indicate that perfective maintenance, apart from the providing of user enhancements, similarly manifests itself in terms of two complementary components.

Relationships in the allocation of time spent in providing user enhancements were also sought. Again, only positive correlation coefficients were judged noteworthy, because of the computational dependency existing. It was found that relative time spent in reformatting existing reports was positively associated with relative time spent in condensing data in existing reports ($r = 0.119$, $s = 0.004$); and relative time spent in condensing data in existing reports was in turn positively associated with relative time spent in consolidating the number of reports ($r = 0.180$, $s = 0.001$). A suggested interpretation is that all three activities are essentially complementary in the enhancement of a system which provides the user with "too much."

The relative development experience of the maintainers of the application system was also significantly related to the magnitude of the maintenance effort. First, both the number of person-hours spent in maintenance and the number of persons assigned were found to be negatively associated with relative development experience ($r = -0.191$, $s = 0.001$; $r = -0.139$, $s = 0.001$). These comparatively strong findings suggest the possibility that development experience may be of importance in maintenance productivity; however, further analysis is necessary to establish this. In particular, it is necessary to assess the influence of system size and age on this possible relationship. (This is discussed on page 84, forthcoming.) Secondly, the allocation of maintenance time to various problem areas was also found to be related to the relative development experience of the maintainers. Both relative time in emergency fixes and relative time in routine debugging were negatively associated with relative development experience ($r = -0.063$, $s = 0.084$; $r = -0.117$, $s = 0.005$); and relative time in recoding for computational efficiency was positively associated ($r = 0.077$, $s = 0.044$). Again, this finding suggests the possible importance of development experience, here in the efficient performance of corrective maintenance, but similarly requires further analysis. (See page 84.) A last related finding was that, in providing user enhancements, the relative time spent in providing additional reports was positively associated with relative development experience (r = 0.091, s = 0.023). However, the correlation is small, and the finding offers no apparent interpretation.

The next major consideration was the relationship between magnitude of the maintenance effort and the size and age of the application system. First-order Pearson correlation coefficients were computed relating both number of maintenance person-hours and number of maintainers assigned, to system age and five measures of system size. The results are shown in Figure 5.6. As expected, all coefficients are positive and significant. All are also of size r 0.100. An interesting question is the extent to which the apparent relationship between system age and the magnitude of the maintenance effort might be explained by the fact that older systems tend to be larger systems (see the results of the previous chapter). Partial correlation coefficients between number of maintenance person-hours and maintainers assigned, and system age were thus computed, controlling for various measures of system size.

It was found that system size does in fact explain part of the relationship between magnitude of the maintenance effort and system age. However, the relationship persists, even when controlled. Not all correlation coefficients remained significant at the s = 0.100 level or better, and few are of size r 0.100, but all remained positive. (See Figure 5.9, at the conclusion of this chapter.)

Also investigated was the relationship between the allocation of the maintenance effort and the size and age of the application system. The first-order Pearson correlation coefficients computed are shown in Figure 5.7. An asterisk identifies those coefficients which are both significant at the level s 0.100 and of magnitude r 0.100. On the whole, larger systems are seen to be associated with a relatively greater effort in routine debugging, and a relatively lesser effort in accommodating data and file changes. The results are mixed for other categories of maintenance activity, and offer no general interpretation. In terms of the allocation of effort in providing user enhancements, larger systems are associated with relatively greater effort in providing new, additional reports, and relatively lesser effort in reformatting existing reports. In particular, systems which provide the greater number of existing reports are seen to be strongly associated with a relatively greater effort in providing new, additional reports. This relationship is perhaps due to variation in application type; those systems which are report generating in nature may be associated with both a greater number of existing reports, and a relatively greater effort in providing new, additional reports.

The age of the application system does not appear to be related to the allocation of the maintenance effort in any substantial way, based on the results shown in Figure 5.7. However, it was judged prudent to test this "non-finding" further, by computing partial correlation coefficients, controlling for those measures of system size significantly involved. Thus, allocation of maintenance effort to routine debugging was correlated to system age, controlling for number of programs, amount of source code, and number of reports. Similarly, allocation of effort to providing user enhancements was correlated to system age, controlling for amount of source code and number of files. In both cases, no significant correlations were found, confirming the absence of a relationship between allocation of maintenance effort and system age.

The finding that larger systems are associated with a relatively greater effort in routine debugging suggests a possible explanation for the earlier finding that the latter is related to a greater level of maintenance effort, on the whole. Partial correlation coefficients were thus computed to test the earlier finding, controlling for application system size. It was found that allocation of effort to routine debugging remained significantly correlated with both number of person-hours allocated to maintenance ($r = 0.126$, $s = 0.007$) and number of persons assigned to maintenance ($r = 0.075$, $s = 0.073$), controlling simultaneously for number of programs, amount of source code, and number of reports. The earlier finding is thus strengthened, and it is concluded that a relatively high proportion of maintenance effort allocated to routine debugging is characteristic of systems requiring a high level of maintenance effort, on the whole.

It is recalled that the relative development experience of the persons maintaining the application system was found to be negatively associated with both total level of effort in maintenance and allocation of effort to routine debugging. (See p. 81.) This suggests that relative development experience might explain the relationship found between the latter two variables. Partial correlation coefficients were computed to investigate this possibility. Controlling for level of development experience, allocation of maintenance effort to routine debugging remained significantly correlated with both number of maintenance person-hours ($r = 0.162$, $s = 0.001$) and number of persons maintaining ($r = 0.122$, $s = 0.009$).

The relationship of relative development experience with total level of effort in maintenance and allocation of effort to routine debugging was itself further investigated, by computing partial correlation coefficients, controlling for system size and age. It was found that the correlations remained significant, at the first three orders of control. It may be concluded that system size and age do not explain the relationship. (See Figure 5.10, at the conclusion of this chapter.)

The relationship established in this subsection must now be integrated and summarized. This requires the synthesis of an explanatory model, relating the relevant variables in a manner both consistent and persuasive, with respect to the findings just discussed. The proposed model is presented in Figure 5.8. Five variables are involved. The dependent variable, amount of maintenance effort, is seen to be influenced through five causal paths involving four other variables. Each causal path is initiated from the independent variable, system age.

The first path in Figure 5.8 is a direct, positive association between system age and amount of maintenance effort. This association was found to be rather weak when other mediating variables of the model are controlled. It may perhaps be explained, in part, by the tendency of a system to become less well-ordered as it ages, and hence harder to repair or enhance, regardless of system size or the skills of the maintainers (see Brooks, 1975).

A second path in Figure 5.8 indicates the tendency of a system to grow in size as it ages, and makes the further obvious association between system size and the amount of maintenance effort demanded.

Less obvious is the causal sequence of a third path, which is the same as the second, except that the relative amount of routine debugging in maintenance mediates between system size and amount of maintenance effort. The existence of this mediating influence is supported by the various correlation coefficients computed, as discussed on pages 82 and 83. These indicated that the relative amount of routine debugging does not vary significantly with system age, but is positively associated with system size. Further, the total amount of maintenance effort is significantly associated with the relative amount of routine debugging, controlling for the other variables in the model. A suggested interpretation is that larger systems tend to demand relatively more routine debugging, because the location and elimination of bugs is a more complex task for larger systems, and because such corrective maintenance is obligatory when needed, and thus receives priority attention. Further, a high relative amount of routine debugging is associated with a high amount of maintenance effort, independent of system size, because it is characteristic of systems which are more troublesome to maintain on the whole.

The last two causal paths shown in Figure 5.8 involve the relative develop ment experience of the individuals maintaining the application system. Both begin with the obvious negative association between system age and relative development experience, i.e., the older the system, the less likely that those persons originally involved in its development will still be associated with it in maintenance. It is then argued that relative development experience is itself negatively associated with the amount of maintenance effort involved, both directly, and indirectly, by means of the mediating variable, relative amount of routine debugging. In the latter case, it is argued that a decrease in relative development experience leads to more relative time spent in routine debugging, which in turn contributes to an increase in the overall amount of the maintenance effort. Each of these relationships is supported by the various correlation coefficients computed. (See pages 81, 83, and 84.)

This completes the analysis of relationships. In the following chapter, the impact of development tools and organizational controls is assessed.

Figure 5.6

Relationships Between Magnitude of Maintenance Effort
and Size and Age of Application System, First-Order
Pearson Correlation Coefficients

	System Age	Programs	Source Code	Files	Data Base Bytes	Reports
Maintenance Person-Hours	0.1504 (443) s=0.001	0.5235 (455) s=0.001	0.5231 (398) s=0.001	0.2074 (451) s=0.001	0.3479 (395) s=0.001	0.4990 (445) s=0.001
Persons Maintaining	0.1799 (453) s=0.001	0.4282 (464) s=0.001	0.4344 (405) s=0.001	0.1512 (461) s=0.001	0.2424 (402) s=0.001	0.3789 (451) s=0.001

Figure 5.7

Relationships Between Allocation of Maintenance Effort and Size and Age of Application System, First-Order Pearson Correlation Coefficients

	System Age	Programs	Source Code	Files	Data Base Bytes	Reports
Emergency Fixes, %	-0.051 (468) s=0.137	-0.016 (479) s=0.368	-0.038 (416) s=0.221	0.023 (477) s=0.309	0.011 (413) s=0.411	-0.038 (465) s=0.207
Routine Debugging, %	-0.000 (468) s=0.499	0.114* (479) s=0.006	0.137* (416) s=0.003	0.044 (477) s=0.167	0.025 (413) s=0.304	0.102* (465) s=0.014
Accom. Data and File Changes, %	0.048 (468) s=0.153	-0.159* (479) s=0.001	-0.121* (416) s=0.007	-0.004 (477) s=0.466	-0.073 (413) s=0.070	-0.040 (465) s=0.196
Accom. Hardware and Software Changes,%	-0.007 (468) s=0.437	0.004 (479) s=0.468	-0.059 (416) s=0.115	0.059 (477) s=0.098	-0.106* (413) s=0.016	-0.042 (465) s=0.185
Enhancements for Users, %	-0.015 (468) s=0.373	-0.003 (479) s=0.471	0.127* (416) s=0.005	-0.107* (477) s=0.010	0.082 (413) s=0.049	0.025 (465) s=0.293
Program Documentation, %	-0.003 (468) s=0.478	0.040 (479) s=0.189	-0.022 (416) s=0.325	0.017 (477) s=0.352	-0.048 (413) s=0.165	-0.020 (465) s=0.332

Figure 5.7 (Continued)

	System Age	Programs	Source Code	Files	Data Base Bytes	Reports
Recoding for Computational Efficiencies, %	-0.024 (468) s=0.300	0.069 (479) s=0.066	0.019 (416) s=0.351	0.108* (477) s=0.009	0.035 (413) s=0.242	0.021 (465) s=0.329
Adding Reports, %	-0.060 (468) s=0.099	0.047 (479) s=0.153	0.081 (416) s=0.050	0.051 (477) s=0.134	0.009 (413) s=0.424	0.191* (465) s=0.001
Adding Data to Existing Reports, %	0.080 (468) s=0.042	-0.049 (479) s=0.142	-0.009 (416) s=0.431	-0.037 (477) s=0.213	0.078 (413) s=0.057	-0.058 (465) s=0.105
Reformatting Existing Reports, %	-0.041 (468) s=0.190	-0.073 (479) s=0.055	-0.125* (416) s=0.005	0.0137 (477) s=0.383	-0.0775 (413) s=0.058	-0.144* (465) s=0.001
Condensing Data in Existing Reports, %	-0.044 (468) s=0.171	-0.005 (479) s=0.457	-0.077 (416) s=0.059	0.014 (477) s=0.380	-0.034 (413) s=0.244	-0.033 (465) s=0.242
Consolidating Reports, %	-0.004 (468) s=0.467	0.061 (479) s=0.091	0.074 (416) s=0.067	0.071 (477) s=0.061	-0.046 (413) s=0.178	0.050 (465) s=0.140

Figure 5.8

Principal Relationships Involving
Magnitude and Allocation of Maintenance Effort

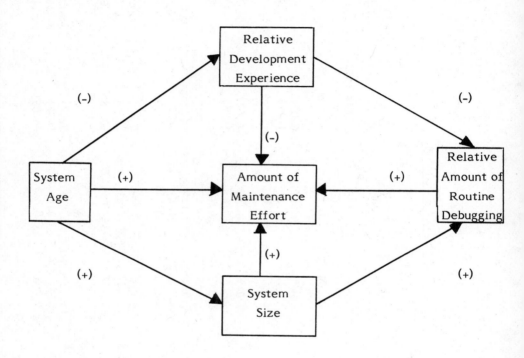

Figure 5.9

Partial Correlation Coefficients for Magnitude
of Maintenance Effort with System Age,
Controlling for System Size

Control Variables	Maintenance Person-hours and System Age	Maintainers Assigned and System Age
Programs (331)	r=0.101 (331) s=0.032	r=0.077 s=0.080
Source Code (331)	r=0.087 (331) s=0.056	r=0.068 s=0.107
Files (331)	r=0.163 (331) s=0.001	r=0.133 s=0.008
Data Base (331)	r=0.135 (331) s=0.007	r=0.111 s=0.022
Reports (331)	r=0.057 (331) s=0.149	r=0.051 s=0.178
Programs, Source Code (330)	r=0.078 (330) s=0.079	r=0.059 s=0.140
Programs, Files (330)	r=0.102 (330) s=0.032	r=0.078 s=0.078
Programs, Data Base (330)	r=0.092 (330) s=0.048	r=0.071 s=0.098
Programs, Reports (330)	r=0.068 (330) s=0.107	r=0.060 s=0.137
Source Code, Files (330)	r=0.089 (330) s=0.052	r=0.070 s=0.100
Source Code, Data Base (330)	r=0.080 (330) s=0.073	r=0.064 s=0.124

Figure 5.9 (Continued)

Control Variables	Maintenance Person-hours and System Age	Maintainers Assigned and System Age
Source Code, Reports (330)	r=0.048 (330) s=0.194	r=0.043 s=0.220
Files, Data Base (330)	r=0.136 (330) s=0.006	r=0.112 s=0.021
Files, Reports (330)	r=0.058 (330) s=0.146	r=0.054 s=0.166
Data Base, Reports (330)	r=0.051 (330) s=0.179	r=0.046 s=0.201
Programs, Source Code, Files	r=0.078 (329) s=0.078	r=0.060 (329) s=0.137
Programs, Source Code, Data Base	r=0.072 (329) s=0.094	r=0.057 (329) s=0.153
Programs, Source Code, Reports	r=0.057 (329) s=0.150	r=0.052 (329) s=0.175
Programs, Files, Data Base	r=0.091 (329) s=0.048	r=0.072 (329) s=0.097
Programs, Files, Reports	r=0.067 (329) s=0.113	r=0.061 (329) s=0.135
Programs, Data Base, Reports	r=0.061 (329) s=0.133	r=0.056 (329) s=0.155
Source Code, Files, Data Base	r=0.082 (329) s=0.069	r=0.066 (329) s=0.117
Source Code, Files, Reports	r=0.048 (329) s=0.190	r=0.045 (329) s=0.206

Figure 5.9 (Continued)

Control Variables	Maintenance Person-hours and System Age	Maintainers Assigned and System Age
Source Code, Data Base, Reports	$r=0.044$ (329) $s=0.214$	$r=0.040$ (329) $s=0.233$
Files, Data Base, Reports	$r=0.050$ (329) $s=0.184$	$r=0.048$ (329) $s=0.193$

Figure 5.10

Partial Correlation Coefficients for Magnitude
and Allocation of Maintenance Effort with
Development Experience, Controlling for System
Size and Age

Control Variables	Maintenance Person-hours and Development Experience	Maintainers Assigned and Development Experience	Routine Debugging and Development Experience
System Age	r=-0.177 (333) s= 0.001	r=-0.099 (333) s= 0.036	r=-0.087 (333) s= 0.056
Programs	r=-0.212 (333) s= 0.001	r=-0.114 (333) s= 0.019	r=-0.090 (333) s= 0.050
Source Code	r=-0.206 (333) s= 0.001	r=-0.109 (333) s= 0.023	r=-0.086 (333) s= 0.059
Data Base	r=-0.182 (333) s= 0.001	r=-0.102 (333) s= 0.031	r=-0.088 (333) s= 0.054
Reports	r=-0.213 (333) s= 0.001	r=-0.117 (333) s= 0.016	r=-0.092 (333) s= 0.046
System Age, Programs	r=-0.194 (332) s= 0.001	r=-0.097 (332) s= 0.039	r=-0.085 (332) s= 0.061
System Age, Source Code	r=-0.191 (332) s= 0.001	r=-0.095 (332) s= 0.042	r=-0.083 (332) ·s= 0.064
System Age, Data Base	r=-0.155 (332) s=-0.002	r=-0.077 (332) s= 0.079	r=-0.081 (332) s= 0.069
System Age, Reports	r=-0.206 (332) s= 0.001	r=-0.107 (332) s= 0.025	r=-0.087 (332) s= 0.056

Figure 5.10 (Continued)

Control Variables	Maintenance Person-hours and Development Experience	Maintainers Assigned and Development Experience	Routine Debugging and Development Experience
Programs, Source Code	r=-0.210 (332) s= 0.001	r=-0.108 (332) s= 0.025	r=-0.086 (332) s= 0.059
Programs, Data Base	r=-0.195 (332) s= 0.001	r=-0.101 (332) s= 0.032	r=-0.087 (332) s= 0.057
Programs, Reports	r=-0.213 (332) s= 0.001	r=-0.113 (332) s= 0.020	r=-0.090 (332) s =0.050
Source Code, Data Base	r=-0.190 (332) s= 0.001	r=-0.098 (332) s= 0.038	r=-0.085 (332) s= 0.061
Source Code, Reports	r=-0.210 (332) s= 0.001	r=-0.108 (332) s= 0.024	r=-0.086 (332) s= 0.058
Data Base, Reports	r=-0.193 (332) s= 0.001	r=-0.101 (332) s= 0.033	r=-0.087 (332) s= 0.056
System Age, Programs, Source Code	r=-0.197 (331) s= 0.001	r=-0.095 (331) s= 0.041	r=-0.083 (331) s= 0.064
System Age, Programs, Data Base	r=-0.179 (331) s= 0.001	r=-0.086 (331) s= 0.058	r=-0.082 (331) s= 0.068
System Age, Programs, Reports	r=-0.203 (331) s= 0.001	r=-0.100 (331) s= 0.034	r=-0.084 (331) s= 0.062
System Age, Source Code, Data Base	r=-0.176 (331) s= 0.001	r=-0.084 (331) s= 0.063	r=-0.083 (331) s= 0.067
System Age, Source Code, Reports	r=-0.205 (331) s= 0.001	r=-0.100 (331) s= 0.034	r=-0.082 (331) s= 0.067

Figure 5.10 (Continued)

Control Variables	Maintenance Person-hours and Development Experience	Maintainers Assigned and Development Experience	Routine Debugging and Development Experience
System Age, Data Base, Reports	r=-0.187 (331) s= 0.001	r=-0.092 (331) s= 0.047	r=-0.083 (331) s= 0.066
Programs, Source Code, Data Base	r=-0.196 (331) s= 0.001	r=-0.099 (331) s= 0.036	r=-0.085 (331) s= 0.062
Programs, Source Code, Reports	r=-0.211 (331) s= 0.001	r=-0.108 (331) s= 0.025	r=-0.086 (331) s= 0.059
Programs, Data Base, Reports	r=-0.197 (331) s= 0.001	r=-0.101 (331) s= 0.033	r=-0.087 (331) s= 0.057
Source Code, Data Base, Reports	r=-0.195 (331) s= 0.001	r=-0.098 (331) s= 0.037	r=-0.085 (331) s= 0.061

CHAPTER
SIX The Impact of Development Tools and Organizational Controls

In this chapter, the analysis of the survey results continues, with an assessment of the impact of development tools and organizational controls on application system maintenance. Following the established format, the findings will first be summarized. Basic descriptive results and an analysis of relationships follow.

6.1   Summary of Findings

The extent of use of various methods, tools, and techniques in the development of the systems maintained was first discussed in Chapter 4. Of the eight productivity techniques listed in the questionnaire, only three were reported as used in the development of 30% or more of the application systems described. None of these equaled 40% or more. None of the other five had a frequency of use as much as 20%. (See Figure 4.9, page 56).

The use of various organizational controls in maintenance proved to be somewhat more widespread. Of nine controls listed, two were used in more than 3/4 of the applications systems described: the logging and documentation of user requests (79%), and the logging and documentation of changes to programs (77%). Two others were used in somewhat more than half of the systems described: a formal retest procedure for program changes (59%), and the logging and documentation of trouble encountered in operational processing (51%). The rest were used less frequently: charge-back of equipment costs (34%), cost justification of user requests (33%), formal audit (32%), personnel cost charge-back (31%), and the batching of program changes according to a predetermined schedule (28%).

Statistical analysis provided little evidence that the use of either development techniques or organizational controls has any substantial impact upon the level of effort in maintenance, for the application systems described.

However, in the allocation of the maintenance effort, the use of development tools did appear to be of significance. Specifically, in the case of six of the eight tools, significantly more effort was allocated to adaptive or perfective maintenance, and, in one instance, significantly less effort to corrective maintenance. On the whole, this is seen as a favorable redistribution of effort. A suggested interpretation is that the use of certain development tools results in a software product of enhanced quality, enabling the maintenance effort to be redirected from corrective to adaptive and perfective work.

In the case of organizational controls, the use of a particular control was in several instances positively associated with a relatively greater effort allocated to the problem area addressed by the control. For example, there was a tendency to log and document user requests, where a relatively greater amount of effort was spent in providing user enhancements. Thus, in these cases, use of the control proves to be symptomatic of the extent of the problem to which it is applied, rather than offering evidence of successfully ameliorating the effort allocated.

One organizational control, the periodic audit, was associated with relatively less time spent on emergency fixes, and more on providing user enhancements, a trade-off which appears very desirable, where it can be achieved.

The use of organizational controls was further found to vary substantially according to the scale of the data processing environment. All nine controls were used more frequently, the larger the annual equipment budget. Further, the frequency of use of charge-back systems rose sharply at the $500,000 per year equipment budget level, which may represent a transition point between growth stages as suggested by Nolan (1973).

6.2   Basic Descriptive Results

Description of the extent of use of development tools has been presented earlier, in Chapter 4. The basic results are shown in Figure 4.9.

Item 2.15 of the questionnaire explores the extent to which various organizational controls were used in the maintenance of the system. The use of such controls is seen as formalizing the maintenance process, and giving the data processing manager more potential control over its outcomes. Results are shown in Figure 6.1. As may be seen, only four of the nine listed controls are used in a majority of cases, and only the logging and documenting of user requests and program changes are used in three-quarters of the cases or more. That only a third of the systems require that user requests be cost justified is somewhat surprising, though it may perhaps be explained by the fact that some requests would typically be for "corrections" involving no changes in prior commitments. The infrequency with which formal audits are periodically conducted is also notable.

Figure 6.1

What organizational controls are established for the maintenance of the application system?

		Absolute Frequency	(Percent)
a.	All user requests for changes to the application system must be logged and documented.	384	(78.9)
b.	All user requests for changes to the application system must be cost justified.	160	(32.9)
c.	All troubles encountered in the operational processing of the application system programs must be logged and documented.	250	(51.3)
d.	All changes to the application programs must be logged and documented.	375	(77.0)
e.	All changes to the application programs must undergo a formal retest procedure.	285	(58.5)
f.	With the exception of emergency fixes, all changes to the application programs are batched for periodic implementation according to a predetermined schedule.	137	(28.1)
g.	A formal audit of the application system is made periodically.	158	(32.4)
h.	Equipment costs associated with operating and maintaining the application system are charged back (in whole or in part) to the user.	163	(33.5)
i.	Personnel costs associated with operating and maintaining the application system are charged back (in whole or in part) to the user.	150	(30.8)

6.3   Analysis of Relationships

In the previous chapter, the magnitude and allocation of the system maintenance effort was investigated, primarily in terms of its variance according to system age, size, and the development experience of the maintainers. Here this analysis is extended, to consider the impact of the use of development tools and organizational controls on the maintenance effort. The impact of the use of data base management systems is also considered.

Multiple regression analyses provided a primary means of investigation. Number of maintenance person-hours reported and number of persons assigned to maintenance (see Questionnaire Items 2.11 and 2.14) were employed as dependent variables; and system age, size, relative development experience, and the use of a data base management system, various development tools, and organizational controls were employed as independent variables. The latter usage variables were represented as binary scaled, according to the answers to the respective questionnaire items (see Items 2.3, 2.10, and 2.15).

In initial runs, a simple step-wise technique was employed, allowing the independent variables to enter the equations, according to their respective explanatory power at each step. It was expected that one or more measures of system size would enter first on this basis, and that the relative contribution of the use of development tools, organizational controls, and a DBMS would be fairly assessed by controlling for system size in this fashion. A minimum F-statistic value of 1.0 was required for the entry of a variable into the regression equations. Setting the value at this level permitted an extended consideration of the behavior of the variables of interest, yet provided an effective cut-off with respect to the analysis as a whole.

The reader is reminded that in the multiple regression analyses, as in analyses described earlier, the natural logarithm transformation of the system size variables and the two variables describing the magnitude of the maintenance effort are used.

The first step-wise analysis employed number of annual maintenance person-hours as the dependent variable. Results of the analysis are shown in the Summary Table of Figure 6.2. As expected, measures of system size dominate the explanatory equation. A multiple regression coefficient of R = 0.705 is achieved on the whole, which is equivalent to accounting for approximately 50% of the variation in number of maintenance person-hours. Number of programs, number of source statements, and number of data base bytes enter the equation first, and account for a multiple R = 0.637. System development experience (negatively associated), the use of a data base manage ment system, and the number of reports enter next, and raise the multiple R to a value of 0.674. Note that the simple correlation coefficient for the number of reports is relatively high; the explanatory value of this variable is reduced by the prior entry of the other size variables into the equation. Note also the positive association of the use of a data base management system, controlling for the size of the application system and the development experience of the staff. Evidently, whatever advantages are associated with the use of a DBMS, reduction of the maintenance task may not be among them.

Continuing with the initial analysis summarized in Figure 6.2, it is seen that the use of five development tools and four organizational controls enter the regression equation, within the cut-off level of F = 1.0. Positively associated with number of maintenance person-hours are: automated flow charting, the batching of program changes, the operations trouble log, structured programming, equipment cost charge-back, the data base dictionary, and structured walk-through. Negatively associated are: chief programmer team, user request justification, and decision tables. In each case, the direction of association is the same as that of the simple correlation coefficient. Not associated are two development tools and five organizational controls: test data generators, HIPO, the user request log, the program change log, program change retest procedure, periodic audit, and personnel cost charge-back. Also not associated is system age. On the whole, then, there is little evidence to suggest that the use of development tools and organizational controls contributes to a reduction in the number of person-hours required to maintain an application system.

Figure 6.2

Multiple Regression

Dependent Variable: Number of Maintenance Person-Hours

		Summary Table			
Independent Variables	Multiple R	R Square	RSQ Change	Simple R	Beta
Ln of Programs	0.562	0.315	0.315	0.562	0.152
Ln of Source Code	0.612	0.375	0.059	0.558	0.228
Ln of Data Base	0.637	0.406	0.031	0.415	0.161
Development Experience	0.655	0.429	0.023	-0.210	-0.158
DBMS	0.666	0.443	0.014	0.221	0.082
Ln of Reports	0.674	0.454	0.011	0.527	0.175
Automated Flowcharting	0.680	0.463	0.009	0.133	0.092
Program Changes Batched	0.685	0.469	0.006	0.142	0.064
Chief Programmer Team	0.688	0.473	0.004	-0.035	-0.094
Operations Trouble Log	0.692	0.478	0.005	0.251	0.078
User Request Justification	0.695	0.483	0.005	-0.019	-0.082
Structured Programming	0.699	0.489	0.005	0.054	0.072
Equipment Cost Charge-Back	0.701	0.491	0.003	0.205	0.054
Decision Tables	0.702	0.493	0.002	-0.074	-0.054
Data Base Dictionary	0.703	0.495	0.002	0.176	0.046
Structured Walk-Through	0.705	0.496	0.002	0.034	0.045

The second step-wise analysis employed number of persons maintaining the application system as the dependent variable to be explained. Since this variable is somewhat more crude as a measure of the maintenance effort, the explanatory relationship may be expected to be somewhat weaker, as indeed is the case. Results are summarized in Figure 6.3. A multiple R = 0.602 is achieved. As before, number of programs and number of source statements enter the regression equation first, accounting in this case for a multiple R = 0.499. After this, the pattern of entry of the variables varies somewhat from the previous analysis. Number of data base bytes enters somewhat later, and number of reports enters not at all. System development experience also enters somewhat later, though the negative association remains. The use of a DBMS enters as before with a significant positive association. System age enters weakly as the last variable, positively associated.

A total of three tools and four organizational controls enter the regression equation summarized in Figure 6.3, at the F = 1.0 cut-off level. Positively associated, as with the previous analysis, are automated flow-charting, the operations trouble log, structured programming, equipment cost charge-back, and the data base dictionary. Also positively associated is the program change retest procedure. Negatively associated, as before, is the user request justification. Of all the development tools and organizational controls, this is the only one to achieve a negative association and inclusion in both of the regression runs. However, this negative association is very weak.

Also of interest is the extent to which the allocation of the maintenance effort is related to the use of development tools. In general, maintenance may be classified into three types: corrective (emergency program fixes, routine debugging); adaptive (accommodation of changes to data inputs and files, and to hardware and system software); and perfective (enhancements for users, improvement of program documentation, recoding for efficiency in computation). (Swanson, 1976) Within this classification, the demands for corrective work are likely to have precedence over those for adaptive work, which are in turn likely to have precedence over demands for perfective work. Thus, where the demands for corrective maintenance are substantial, resources for adaptive and, in particular, perfective maintenance, become more scarce, an undesirable situation.

Figure 6.3

Multiple Regression
Dependent Variable: Number of Maintainers of System

Summary Table

Independent Variables	Multiple R	R Square	RSQ Change	Simple R	Beta
Ln of Programs	0.464	0.216	0.216	0.464	0.227
Ln of Source Code	0.499	0.249	0.034	0.448	0.185
Automated Flowcharting	0.531	0.282	0.033	0.231	0.170
Operations Trouble Log	0.554	0.307	0.025	0.260	0.118
DBMS	0.564	0.318	0.011	0.190	0.064
Retest Procedure	0.571	0.327	0.008	0.153	0.090
Ln of Data Base	0.577	0.333	0.007	0.292	0.069
Structured Programming	0.583	0.340	0.007	0.110	0.093
Development Experience	0.588	0.346	0.006	-0.129	-0.072
Equipment Cost Charge-Back	0.593	0.352	0.005	0.207	0.088
Data Base Dictionary	0.597	0.356	0.004	0.187	0.074
User Request Justification	0.600	0.360	0.004	0.017	-0.065
System Age, Months	0.602	0.363	0.003	0.136	0.058

One-way analyses of variance of the allocation of the maintenance effort according to the use of productivity aids were thus performed. Results are summarized in Figure 6.4. Nine significant relationships are established. With one exception, these relationships reflect favorably on the use of productivity aids. Corrective maintenance is relatively less in one instance, adaptive maintenance is relatively greater in two instances, and perfective maintenance is relatively greater in five instances. Only in the case of automated flowcharting is the evidence unfavorable.

A suggested interpretation is that the overall level of maintenance remains the same, whether productivity aids were used in development or not. However, resources are freed somewhat from corrective maintenance, and redirected to adaptive and perfective maintenance. This should be possible if the software product developed is of higher quality, i.e., it contains fewer errors, and/or is more easy to repair when necessary. In the next chapter, some confirming evidence of this interpretation is provided.

One-way analyses of variance of the allocation of maintenance effort according to the use of organization controls were also performed. A summary of the statistically significant results is shown in Figure 6.5. In several instances, the use of a particular control is found to be positively associated with the allocation of maintenance effort to the problem area addressed by the control. For example, the use of a user request log is positively associated with allocating effort to providing user enhancements, and the use of an operations trouble log is positively associated with allocating effort to routine debugging. In these cases, the use of a control proves to be symptomatic of the extent of the problem to which it is applied, rather than offering evidence of successfully ameliorating the effort allocated. Perhaps the most interesting finding is that associated with the use of a periodic audit. Here it is found that relatively less time is spent on emergency fixes, and more on providing user enhancements, a situation presumably agreeable to all concerned.

Also of interest is the extent to which organizational controls tend to be used collectively, or independently. First-order Pearson correlation coefficients provide adequate indicators of association in this regard, without

Figure 6.4

Analyses of Variance of Allocation of
Maintenance Effort by Use of Development Tools

Decision Tables

    Recoding for computational efficiency   (+) $s=0.0001$

Data Base Dictionary

    (None)

Test Data Generators

    Accommodation of system hardware and

    software changes   (+) $s=0.075$

Structured Programming

    Emergency fixes   (−) $s=0.037$

    Recoding for computational efficiency   (+) $s=0.086$

Automated Flowcharting

    User enhancements   (−) $s=0.061$

HIPO

    User enhancements   (+) $s=0.007$

Structured Walk-Through

    User enhancements   (+) $s=0.023$

    Recoding for computational efficiency   (+) $s=0.084$

Chief Programmer Team

    Accommodation of system hardware and

    software changes   (+) $s=0.076$

NOTE: (+)   Indicates mean allocation percentage higher for use of tool;
          (−)   indicates mean allocation percentage lower for use of tool.

Figure 6.5

Analysis of Variance of Allocation of
Maintenance Effort by Use of Organizational Controls

User Request Log
  User enhancements   (+) $s=0.011$
  Recoding for computational efficiency   (+) $s=0.080$

User Request Justification
  Program documentation   (+) $s=0.034$

Operations Trouble Log
  Routine debugging   (+) $s=0.039$

Program Change Log
  Routine debugging   (+) $s=0.045$
  Recoding for computational efficiency   (+) $s=0.032$

Program Change Retest Procedure
  Accommodation of system hardware and
  software changes   (+) $s=0.090$
  Program documentation   (+) $s=0.022$

Batching of Program Changes
  Routine debugging   (+) $s=0.081$
  Accommodation of system hardware and
  software changes   (+) $s=0.014$

Periodic Audit
  Emergency fixes   (-) $s=0.027$
  User enhancements   (+) $s=0.052$

Equipment Cost Charge-Back
  Accommodation of system hardware and
  software changes   (+) $s=0.092$
  User enhancements   (+) $s=0.068$
  Program documentation   (-) $s=0.061$

Personnel Cost Charge-Back
  Accommodation of system hardware and   (+) $s=0.058$
  software changes

NOTE: (+) Indicates mean allocation percentage higher for use of controls;
      (-) Indicates mean allocation percentage lower for use of control.

resorting to cross-tabular analysis. These are presented in Figure 6.6. All coefficients are positive, confirming that the controls include no substitutes. The strongest association is between the use of equipment cost charge-back and personnel cost charge-back (r = 0.809). Other notable associations are between the user request log and the program change log (r = 0.541); the user request log and the operations trouble log (r = 0.391); and the program change log and the operations trouble log (r = 0.317). Thus, when costs are charged back, both equipment and personnel tend to be included. Similarly, the use of various logs as organizational controls appears to be complementary. Two other associations are between the batching of program changes and the periodic audit (r = 0.181); and the program change log and the program change retest procedure (r = 0.233).

It is to be expected that the use of organizational controls would vary substantially according to the size of the data processing organization, as represented by the equipment budget. Cross-tabular analyses were performed to investigate this hypothesis. It was found that all nine tools tended significantly to be used the more frequently, the larger the equipment budget. Results are summarized in Figure 6.7. Note that in the case of equipment and personnel cost charge-backs, usage doubles in frequency at the $500K budget breaking point. This may perhaps represent a point of transition between stages of growth, as described by Nolan (1973).

This completes the analysis for the present chapter. The chapter to follow addresses the problems of maintenance.

Figure 6.6

Use of Organizational Controls, First-Order Pearson
Correlation Coefficients

	1. User Request Log	2. User Request Justification	3. Operations Trouble Log	4. Program Change Log	5. Program Change Retest	6. Program Changes Batched	7. Periodic Audit	8. Equip-Cost Charge-Back	9. Personnel Cost Charge-Back
1	1.0000 (487) P=******	0.0946 (487) P=0.018	0.3911 (487) P=0.000	0.5414 (487) P=0.000	0.1355 (487) P=0.001	0.1451 (487) P=0.001	0.1441 (487) P=0.001	0.1755 (487) P=0.000	0.1277 (487) P=0.002
2	0.0946 (487) P=0.018	1.0000 (487) P=******	0.1038 (487) P=0.011	0.0914 (487) P=0.022	0.1009 (487) P=0.013	0.0777 (487) P=0.043	0.1036 (487) P=0.011	0.0875 (487) P=0.027	0.105 (487) P=0.013
3	0.3911 (487) P=0.000	0.1038 (487) P=0.011	1.0000 (487) P=******	0.3172 (487) P=0.000	0.1726 (487) P=0.000	0.1706 (487) P=0.000	0.1658 (487) P=0.000	0.1421 (487) P=0.001	0.1424 (487) P=0.001
4	0.5414 (487) P=0.000	0.0914 (487) P=0.022	0.3172 (487) P=0.000	1.0000 (487) P=******	0.2332 (487) P=0.000	0.1466 (487) P=0.001	0.2120 (487) P=0.000	0.1188 (487) P=0.004	0.0792 (487) P=0.040

Figure 6.6 (Continued)

	1	2	3	4	5	6	7	8	9
5	0.1355 (487) P=0.001	0.1009 (487) P=0.013	0.1726 (487) P=0.000	0.2332 (487) P=0.000	1.0000 (487) P=*****	0.0911 (487) P=0.022	0.1650 (487) P=0.000	0.0495 (487) P=0.138	0.0200 (487) P=0.330
6	0.1451 (487) P=0.001	0.0777 (487) P=0.043	0.1706 (487) P=0.000	0.1466 (487) P=0.001	0.0911 (487) P=0.022	1.0000 (487) P=*****	0.1810 (487) P=0.000	0.1175 (487) P=0.005	0.0871 (487) P=0.027
7	0.1441 (487) P=0.001	0.1036 (487) P=0.011	0.1658 (487) P=0.000	0.2120 (487) P=0.000	0.1650 (487) P=0.000	0.1810 (487) P=0.000	1.0000 (487) P=*****	0.0476 (487) P=0.147	0.0412 (487) P=0.182
8	0.1755 (487) P=0.000	0.0875 (487) P=0.027	0.1421 (487) P=0.001	0.1188 (487) P=0.004	0.0495 (487) P=0.138	0.1175 (487) P=0.005	0.0476 (487) P=0.147	1.0000 (487) P=*****	0.8087 (487) P=0.000
9	0.1277 (487) P=0.002	0.1015 (487) P=0.013	0.1424 (487) P=0.001	0.0792 (487) P=0.040	0.0200 (487) P=0.330	0.0871 (487) P=0.027	0.0412 (487) P=0.182	0.8087 (487) P=0.000	1.0000 (487) P=*****

Figure 6.7: Frequency of Use of Organizational Controls
by Data Processing Equipment Budget

Annual Data Processing Equipment Budget

Use of Organizational Controls	Less Than $125K	$125K-250K	$250K-500K	$500K-1M	$1M-2M	$2M-4M	$4M or More	Totals	Statistical Significance Levels*
User Requests Logged and Documented	86 (61.0%)	62 (76.5%)	59 (83.1%)	65 (90.3%)	48 (92.3%)	26 (96.3%)	32 (91.4%)	378 (78.9%)	0.000, 0.000
User Requests Cost Justified	38 (27.0%)	28 (34.6%)	27 (38.0%)	24 (33.3%)	18 (34.6%)	12 (44.4%)	12 (34.3%)	159 (33.2%)	0.081, 0.052
Operations Troubles Logged and Documented	46 (32.6%)	36 (44.4%)	38 (53.5%)	44 (61.1%)	33 (63.5%)	21 (77.8%)	26 (74.3%)	244 (50.9%)	0.000, 0.000
Program Changes Logged and Documented	96 (68.1%)	62 (76.5%)	56 (78.9%)	60 (83.3%)	42 (80.8%)	22 (81.5%)	31 (88.6%)	369 (77.0%)	0.074, 0.001
Formal Retest Procedure	70 (49.6%)	51 (63.0%)	36 (50.7%)	47 (65.3%)	28 (53.8%)	18 (66.7%)	29 (82.9%)	279 (58.2%)	0.006, 0.002
Changes Batched and Scheduled	31 (22.0%)	22 (27.2%)	18 (25.4%)	28 (38.9%)	16 (30.8%)	7 (25.9%)	14 (40.0%)	136 (28.4%)	0.005, 0.009

Figure 6.7: (Continued)

Annual Data Processing Equipment Budget

Use of Organizational Controls	Less Than $125K	$125K-250K	$250K-500K	$500K--1M	$1M-2M	$2M-4M	$4M or More	Totals	Statistical Significance Levels*
Formal Periodic Audit	34 (24.1%)	21 (25.9%)	28 (39.4%)	25 (34.7%)	19 (36.5%)	16 (59.3%)	13 (37.1%)	156 (32.6%)	0.008, 0.001
Equipment Cost Charge-back	27 (19.1%)	20 (24.7%)	16 (22.5%)	34 (47.2%)	27 (51.9%)	17 (63.0%)	19 (54.3%)	160 (33.4%)	0.000, 0.000
Personnel Cost Charge-back	27 (19.1%)	15 (18.5%)	13 (18.3%)	33 (45.8%)	27 (51.9%)	14 (51.9%)	17 (48.6%)	146 (30.5%)	0.000, 0.000

*Only signifance levels less than 0.100 are shown. The first level in each pair corresponds to the raw chi-square statistic. The second is Kendall's Tau B.

CHAPTER SEVEN The Problems of Maintenance

In this chapter, the analysis of the survey results concludes with an assessment of the problems of maintenance. This assessment is based principally on the respondents' answers to Item 2.16 of the questionnaire.

Following the usual format, a summary of the findings is presented first, followed by basic descriptive results and an analysis of relationships.

7.1 Summary of Findings

The final series of results pertain to data processing management's assessment of various problems in maintaining the application system described. Twenty-six potential problems were rated by the respondents on a 1 to 5 point scale ranging from "no problem at all" to "major problem." The six problems seen as most severe were: quality of application system documentation, user demand for enhancements and extensions; competing demands for maintenance programmer personnel time; meeting scheduled commitments; inadequate training of user personnel; and turnover in user organization. Each of these was at least a "minor problem" in the maintenance of more than half the systems described and at least a "somewhat major" problem for more than a fourth of these systems.

Of the six problems seen as most severe, three are concerned with users of the application system, two involve managerial constraints associated with time availability, and one, dealing with documentation, is of a more technical nature. On the whole, the predominance of non-technical over technical problems is striking, emphasizing the need to address managerial issues in maintenance.

The underlying dimensions of the problem assessments were also determined, by statistical analysis. Six problem factors were identified. The most dominant was that of user knowledge, which was found to account for about 60% of the common variance in the problem assessments. The dimension of programmer effectiveness was a distant second in importance, accounting for 12% of the problem variance. Other dimensions identified were those of product quality, programmer time availability, machine requirements, and system reliability. None of these accounted for as much as 10% of the problem variance.

Statistical analysis showed the problems in maintenance, as represented by the six problem factors identified, to be significantly associated with various other characteristics of the maintenance process, the application system maintained, and the data processing environment. These associations will now be summarized, in conclusion.

A first association relates to system size and age. Larger and older systems were found associated with greater problems in maintenance, on the average. Each problem factor was represented in this pattern of associations, although two, programmer effectiveness and product quality, seemed most strongly associated. Subsequent analysis also provided an explanation of these associations, in terms of other, intervening variables.

116

The magnitude and allocation of the effort in maintenance were also found associated with the perceived problems. As might be expected, the problems were perceived to be greater, the greater the magnitude of the maintenance effort, as measured by both annual person-hours and individuals assigned. All six problem factors were represented, with programmer effectiveness and product quality showing the most significant associations.

Problems of maintenance were also perceived to be the greater, the more relative time is spent in the corrective form of maintenance. Here, notable associations involved problems of programmer effectiveness, product quality, and user knowledge.

Interestingly, no notable findings related the allocation of maintenance time to providing user enhancements to any of the problems of maintenance, including that of user knowledge.

The relative development experience of the maintainers of the application system, as measured by the relative fraction who had actually worked on the development of this same system, proved also to be associated with the perceived problems in maintenance. Most significantly associated were problems of product quality and programmer effectiveness, both perceived to be the greater, the less the relative development experience of the maintainers. Greater problems with user knowledge and programmer time availability were also indicated.

As described earlier, the magnitude of the effort in maintenance, the allocation of maintenance time to routine debugging (a form of corrective maintenance), and the relative development experience of the maintainers, are all found to be dependent in part upon the age and/or size of the application system maintained. When the effects of these three dependent variables upon the problems of maintenance have been accounted for, it is found that the relationships between system age and size, and the problems of maintenance are explained.

Statistical analysis also showed the problems of maintenance to be associated with the use of productivity techniques in system development.

Specifically, lesser problems in product quality were found to be associated with the use of test data generators, structured programming, HIPO, structured walk-thorough, and the chief programmer team. This is an encouraging result for the advocates of these techniques. However, it must be noted that the problems of user knowledge and programmer effectiveness, which together account for almost 72% of the common problem variance, remain unaffected.

The use of a data base management system was found to be statistically unrelated to management's perceptions of the problems in maintenance.

Two problem factors varied significantly according to the language in which the application system was programmed: programmer effectiveness and system reliability. Problems with programmer effectiveness appeared, on the whole, to be greater, the more sophisticated the language. For example, such problems were greater, on an average, where FORTRAN, PL/1, or assembler were used, and less, on an average, where RPG was used. However this apparent relationship may well be spurious. Other evidence indicated that more sophisticated languages tend to be used in the larger scale data processing environments and that problems of programmer effectiveness tend to be greater in these environments. For organizations of the same size, no significant relationship was found between choice of programming language and problems of programmer effectiveness.

Problems with system reliability were seen as greater, on average, where FORTRAN was used, and less, on average, where RPG was used. This relationship was not explainable by the scale of the data processing environment.

The use of organizational controls appeared, at first, to be associated with relatively greater problems in system maintenance. However, when the effects of three other variables, viz. number of annual maintenance person-hours, relative allocation of effort to corrective maintenance, and relative development experience of the maintainers are controlled, little relationship between the use of organizational controls and the problems of maintenance was found. An exception was the periodic audit, which was significantly associated with lesser problems of user knowledge and product quality.

As mentioned earlier, the problems of maintenance were also found to vary, according to the scale of the data processing environment. Specifically, the problem of programmer effectiveness was held to be greater on average, the larger the annual data processing equipment budget. However, no significant variances in the other five problem factors existed. Whether smaller organizations actually tend to have greater programmer effectiveness is an open question. An alternative interpretation is that effectiveness does not itself vary, but that awareness of the "problem" is heightened according to the visibility of the data processing budget.

Several other findings relating the perceived problems of maintenance to the data processing environment are also reported. In general, problems in maintaining the system described were seen as greater, where more of the organization's time is allocated to maintenance, on the whole. Similarly, problems were perceived to be greater, the less sufficient the staffing level of the department. Finally, not surprisingly, the more the data processing manager's own time is absorbed by the demands of maintenance, the greater are the problems seen to be.

7.2   Basic Descriptive Results

Item 2.16 concluded the questionnaire, and sought the data processing manager's judgement of the problems in maintaining the application system described. A list of twenty-six potential problems was provided, and it was requested that each be evaluated on a 1 to 6 point scale ranging from "no problem at all" to "major problem."   The list of potential problems was identical to that used in the preliminary survey described earlier (see Section 1.2), with the exception of the last three items, which were added on the basis of comments received in this same first survey.

The results for Item 2.16 are shown in Figure 7.1 and are based upon the assumption of an ordinal item scale, an assumption which will be revised to that of an interval scale, for certain analyses to follow in the next section. The distribution of responses for each problem is portrayed by means of a figure constructed on the basis of median and quartile responses. The peak of this figure represents the median response, and the sides represent the quartiles. Thus, for example, in case of turnover of maintenance personnel, the median response was "somewhat minor problem," and the low and high quartiles were "no problem," respectively.

Six problems are seen to be most severe, in the data processing manager's judgment: quality of application system documentation; user demand for enhancements and extensions to application system; copeting demands for maintenance programmer personnel time; meeting scheduled commitments; inadequate training of user personnel; and turnover in user organization. On the whole, the predominance of non-technical over technical problems is striking.   Of the six problems, three are concerned with the users of the applicatioon system, two are concerned with managerial constraints involving time availability, and one deals with the more technical problem of application system documentation.

The problem seen to be the least severe, in the data processing manager's judgment, is that of system hardwre and software reliability, a purely technical matter in application system maintenance.

Figure 7.1

In your judgment, to what extent are (or have been) the following a problem in maintaining the application system?

Median and Quartile Responses

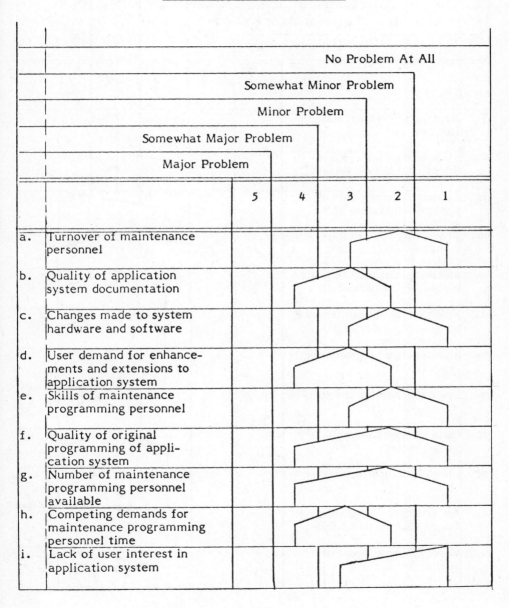

	No Problem At All				
		Somewhat Minor Problem			
			Minor Problem		
	Somewhat Major Problem				
	Major Problem				
	5	4	3	2	1
a. Turnover of maintenance personnel					
b. Quality of application system documentation					
c. Changes made to system hardware and software					
d. User demand for enhancements and extensions to application system					
e. Skills of maintenance programming personnel					
f. Quality of original programming of application system					
g. Number of maintenance programming personnel available					
h. Competing demands for maintenance programming personnel time					
i. Lack of user interest in application system					

Figure 7.1 (Continued)

	5 Major Problem	4 Somewhat Major Problem	3 Minor Problem	2 Somewhat Minor Problem	1 No Problem At All
j.	Application system run failures				
k.	Lack of user understanding of application system				
l.	Storage requirements of application system programs				
m.	Processing time requirements of application system programs				
n.	Motivation of maintenance programming personnel				
o.	Forecasting of maintenance programming personnel requirements				
p.	Maintenance programming productivity				
q.	System hardware and software reliability				
r.	Data integrity in application system				
s.	Unrealistic user expectations				
t.	Adherence to programming standards in maintenance				
u.	Management support of application system				

Figure 7.1 (Continued)

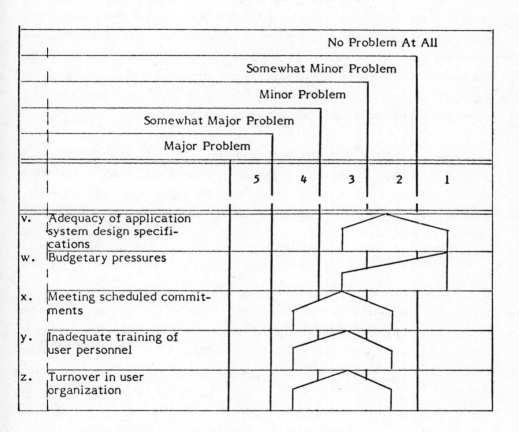

7.3   Analysis of Relationships

In this section, the problems of maintenance are related to other items in the questionnaire.

In Figure 7.1, results were presented based upon the assumption of ordinal item scales. Here the stronger assumption of interval item scales is made for analytic purposes. A summary of the means and standard deviations of the individual problem item distributions is presented in Figure 7.2. Problem items are listed in the order they are listed in the questionnaire. In general, the means and standard deviations portray the distributions much as in Figure 7.1. However, user demands for enhancements and extensions does emerge as clearly the leading problem among all those listed.

A factor analysis of the responses to the twenty-six problem items was performed, in order to explore the underlying dimensionality, and to facilitate further analysis. The principal factor with iteration option was employed, with varimax rotation. (Nie et al., 1975). A classical factor analysis, based on inferred factors, was thus performed. The method of rotation chosen was the common one.

The factor analysis produced six factors which accounted for the common variance in the twenty six problem items. Those factors are summarized in Figure 7.3. The labels attached to the factors are the result of an interpretation of the factor score coefficients shown in Figure 7.4. These coefficients indicate the relative contributions of the problem items to the factor scores computed. To provide a guide to the interpretation, coefficients of noteworthy size are identified with asterisks (see the key to the figure). Remarkably, the interpretation proves to be rather straightforward.

It is seen that five of the six factor coefficients marked with an asterisk under Factor 1 identify problem items which refer specifically to the users of the information system. The sixth, which refers to "management support," may also be given a user-related interpretation. Factor 1, which accounts for 59.5% of the common variance in the responses to all twenty six problem items, may thus be reasonably labeled the problem of "user knowledge," based

Figure 7.2

Distribution of Maintenance Problem Items

Variables	Labels	Mean	Standard Dev.	Cases
MNPROB1	Maintenance personnel turnover	2.2332	1.3356	446
MNPROB2	Documentation quality	3.0000	1.3103	446
MNPROB3	System hardware and software changes	2.0404	1.1739	446
MNPROB4	Demand for enhancements and extensions	3.2018	1.1745	446
MNPROB5	Skills of maintenance programmers	2.0807	1.1564	446
MNPROB6	Quality of original programming	2.5897	1.3256	446
MNPROB7	Number of maintenance programmers available	2.5762	1.3348	446
MNPROB8	Competing demands for programmer time	3.0336	1.3395	446
MNPROB9	Lack of user interest	1.8677	1.2171	446
MNPROB10	System run failures	1.8677	0.9706	446
MNPROB11	Lack of user understanding	2.6076	1.2670	446
MNPROB12	Program storage requirements	1.9776	1.2158	446
MNPROB13	Program processing time requirements	2.5538	1.2562	446
MNPROB14	Maintenance programmer motivation	1.9170	1.1076	446

125

Figure 7.2 (Continued)

Variables	Labels	Mean	Standard Dev.	Cases
MNPROB15	Forecasting maintenance programming requirements	2.4552	1.2239	446
MNPROB16	Maintenance programming productivity	2.0359	1.0866	446
MNPROB17	System hardware and software reliability	1.8094	1.0438	446
MNPROB18	Data integrity	1.9036	1.0840	446
MNPROB19	Unrealistic user expectations	2.5516	1.2616	446
MNPROB20	Adherence to programming standards	2.1143	1.0905	446
MNPROB21	Management support	1.8453	1.1141	446
MNPROB22	Adequacy of system design specifications	2.4283	1.2606	446
MNPROB23	Budgetary pressures	1.9798	1.2075	446
MNPROB24	Meeting scheduled commitments	2.6861	1.2435	446
MNPROB25	Inadequate user training	2.7623	1.2387	446
MNPROB26	Turnover in user organization	2.3610	1.2351	446

Figure 7.3

Summary of Maintenance Problem Factors

Label	Eigenvalue	% of Var.	Cum. %
User knowledge	7.25414	59.5	59.5
Programmer effectiveness	1.45230	11.9	71.4
Product quality	1.16047	9.5	80.9
Programmer time availability	0.97415	8.0	88.9
Machine requirement	0.76567	6.8	95.2
System reliability	0.58859	4.8	100.0

Figure 7.4

Problem Factor Coefficients

Variable	Factor 1	Factor 2	Factor 3	Factor 4	Factor 5	Factor 6
MNPROB1	-0.04521	0.10695*	0.02156	0.00674	-0.05779	0.06764
MNPROB2	-0.06644	-0.03852	0.27184**	0.00110	-0.00582	0.00955
MNPROB3	-0.00943	-0.01415	-0.00699	-0.01810	0.01991	0.17333*
MNPROB4	0.05118	0.02152	-0.01526	0.02296	0.03172	-0.02123
MNPROB5	-0.08622	0.22730**	0.03759	-0.03784	-0.02746	0.04512
MNPROB6	-0.08716	-0.01115	0.32069**	-0.04889	-0.01086	0.01871
MNPROB7	-0.03169	0.07115	-0.00522	0.14772*	-0.01257	-0.02537
MNPROB8	-0.06997	-0.17608*	-0.01721	0.78537**	-0.02472	-0.00635
MNPROB9	0.13855*	-0.01215	0.02271	-0.05349	-0.01204	-0.09485
MNPROB10	-0.02340	-0.02459	0.10837*	-0.02321	-0.00812	0.15754*
MNPROB11	0.36301**	-0.10578*	-0.02331	-0.07230	0.01735	-0.09868
MNPROB12	-0.03805	-0.01484	-0.01234	-0.02045	0.47591**	-0.03657
MNPROB13	-0.03105	-0.02690	-0.01227	-0.01694	0.47141**	0.06795
MNPROB14	-0.01147	0.34931**	-0.04861	-0.09634	0.00968	-0.10137*

Figure 7.4 (Continued)

Variable	Factor 1	Factor 2	Factor 3	Factor 4	Factor 5	Factor 6
MNPROB15	0.03589	0.14128*	-0.10887*	0.10180*	-0.00025	-0.04935
MNPROB16	-0.02935	0.36939**	-0.10989*	-0.08001	0.03882	-0.02649
MNPROB17	-0.07293	-0.01827	-0.00941	-0.02913	-0.02346	0.43967**
MNPROB18	0.05905	-0.01681	0.03245	-0.03812	-0.08623	0.22349**
MNPROB19	0.17311*	-0.04776	-0.02467	0.03369	-0.04264	0.00607
MNPROB20	-0.01215	0.06375	0.07826	-0.00841	0.01669	0.02722
MNPROB21	0.15589*	-0.00798	-0.00157	-0.02836	0.02734	-0.05526
MNPROB22	0.03377	-0.07672	0.40420**	-0.02800	-0.02223	-0.16507*
MNPROB23	0.07904	-0.00187	-0.02341	0.01213	0.00309	0.00032
MNPROB24	0.05503	0.03677	0.03999	0.07347	0.02871	-0.05145
MNPROB25	0.23669*	-0.04170	-0.12469*	0.00565	-0.04806	0.11472*
MNPROB26	0.12929	0.00949	-0.12001*	0.00232	-0.05121	0.13258*

Key:
* Indicates absolute value of coefficient equal to or greater than .100, but less than .200.
** Indicates absolute value of coefficient equal to or greater than .200.

129

in particular upon the two largest factor coefficients, which refer to "lack of user understanding" and "inadequate user training." The labeling of the five other factors follows similar lines of reasoning, and provides no major difficulties in interpretation.

On the whole, the results of the factor analysis are striking. The dimensions emerge with unexpected clarity, and the dominance of the oft cited "user problem" is remarkable. It is not simply that user problems are common to all; it is that user problems account for the major variance in the problems common to all. Note in particular that problem Item 4, "user demand for enhancements and extensions," while it is the major problem item among all those cited, does not appear as a significant component in Factor 1.

For purposes of subsequent analysis, the six problem factors were formalized as indices, computed on the basis of problem items with factor coefficients of absolute value 0.200 or greater. Normalized values of the problem item scores were used in the indices, as recommended. (Nie et al., 1975). A summary of the six factor indices and their problem item components is presented in Figure 7.5.

The remainder of the analysis in this chapter is concerned with relationships involving the six problem factors.

A first relationship established was that problems of maintenance tend to be perceived as greater, the larger the application system being maintained. First-order Pearson correlation coefficients between the six problem factors and five measures of system size are shown in Figure 7.6. Of the 30 coefficients computed, 26 are positive, of which 22 are significant at the $s \leq 0.100$ level, and 14 are of magnitude $|r| \geq 0.100$. The problem factor "programmer effectiveness" demonstrates a notable positive association with all five measures of system size. The factor "product quality" is similarly associated with four of the five size measures. The factor "user knowledge" is notably associated with two of the size measures, and the remaining three factors are similarly associated with one size measure each.

Figure 7.5

Problem Factor Indices and Their Item Components

1. User knowledge

11. Lack of user understanding (.363)

25. Inadequate user training (.237)

2. Programmer effectiveness

16. Maintenance programming productivity (.369)

14. Maintenance programming motivation (.349)

5. Skills of maintenance programmers (.227).

3. Product Quality

22. Adequacy of system design specs (.404)

6. Quality of original programming (.321)

2. Documentation quality (.272)

4. Programmer Time Availability

8. Competing demands for programmer time (.785)

5. Machine Requirements

12. Program storage requirements (.476)

13. Program processing time requirements (.471)

6. System Reliability

17. System hardware and software reliability (.440)

18. Data integrity (.223)

NOTE: Factor score coefficients shown in parentheses.

Figure 7.6

Maintenance Problem Factors and System Size:
First-Order Pearson Correction Coefficients

	Programs	Source Code	Files	Database Bytes	Reports
PFACTOR 1 (User Knowledge)	0.1296* (469) P=0.002	0.0521 (409) P=0.147	0.0726 (466) P=0.059	-0.0128 (406) P=0.398	0.1311* (457) P=0.003
PFACTOR 2 (Programmer Effectiveness)	0.1538* (464) P=0.000	0.2027** (405) P=0.000	0.1195* (461) P=0.005	0.1811* (402) P=0.000	0.1427* (452) P=0.001
PFACTOR 3 (Product Quality)	0.1050* (467) P=0.012	0.0913 (409) P=0.033	0.1224* (464) P=0.004	0.1322* (405) P=0.004	0.1069* (454) P=0.011
PFACTOR 4 (Programmer Time Availability)	0.0724 (471) P=0.058	0.0497 (411) P=0.158	-0.0107 (468) P=0.408	0.1086* (408) P=0.014	0.0787 (458) P=0.046
PFACTOR 5 (Machine Requirements)	0.0830 (470) P=0.036	-0.0149 (411) P=0.382	0.1231* (467) P=0.004	0.0090 (408) P=0.428	-0.0242 (457) P=0.303
PFACTOR 6 (System Reliability)	0.0609 (469) P=0.094	0.0750 (410) P=0.065	0.1187* (466) P=0.005	0.0658 (408) P=0.092	0.0264 (456) P=0.287

Key
* Indicates $0.100 \leq r \leq 0.200$
** Indicates $r \geq 0.200$

132

Older systems tend also to be perceived as having greater problems in maintenance. In particular, system age is positively and notably associated with problems of product quality (r = 0.142, s = 0.001) and programmer effectiveness (r = 0.128, s = 0.003). A statistically significant association with the problem of system reliability also exists, but the magnitude of the correlation is not notable. No association exists with the other three problem factors, including that of "user knowledge."

Though system size and age are seen to be strongly associated with the problems of maintenance, this association will be shown in subsequent analysis to be explainable in terms of other intervening variables.

The relative development experience of the maintainers of the application system has been found in earlier analysis to be significant in accounting for the magnitude and allocation of the maintenance effort. The computation of first-order Pearson correlation coefficients show it also to be significantly related to the problems in maintaining the system. The most significant relationships indicate greater development experience to be associated with lesser problems with product quality (r = -0.270, s = 0.001) and lesser problems with programmer effectiveness (r = -0.171, s = 0.001). These results, combined with the earlier, suggest that relative development experience is an important source of productivity in application system maintenance. Lesser problems with user knowledge and programmer time availability were also indicated for higher levels of relative development experience, but correlation coefficients were not of magnitude $|r| \geq 0.100$. Greater problems with machine requirements were indicated (r = 0.104, s = 0.011), for which there is no obvious interpretation. No relationship to the problem of system reliability existed.

Based upon the relationships established thus far, it should be expected that the problems of maintenance would tend also to be the greater, the greater the magnitude of the effort in maintenance. This is indeed the case, as the first-order Pearson correlation coefficients in Figure 7.7 confirm. All twelve coefficients are positive, eleven of these are statistically significant at the $s \leq 0.100$ level and eight are of notable magnitude $|r| \geq 0.0100$. The correlations between number of maintenance person-hours and the problems of

Figure 7.7

Maintenance Problem Factors and Magnitude of Maintenance Effort
First-Order Pearson Correlation Coefficients

	Annual Person-hours	Personnel Assigned
PFACTOR 1	0.1158*	0.0965
(User Knowledge)	(451)	(461)
	P=0.007	P=0.019
PFACTOR 2	0.2625**	0.2088**
(Programmer	(447)	(456)
Effectiveness)	P=0.000	P=0.000
PFACTOR 3	0.2404*	0.1099*
(Product Quality)	(449)	(459)
	P=0.000	P=0.009
PFACTOR 4	0.1445*	0.0879
(Programmer Time	(453)	(462)
Availability)	P=0.001	P=0.029
PFACTOR 5	0.0949	0.0502
(Machine Requirements)	(452)	(462)
	P=0.022	P=0.141
PFACTOR 6	0.1372*	0.1186*
(System Reliability)	(452)	(461)
	P=0.002	P=0.005

Key
*   Indicates $0.100 \leq r \leq 0.200$
**   Indicates $|r| > 0.200$

programmer effectiveness (r = 0.263) and product quality (r = 0.240) are particularly striking.

Another interesting question is the extent to which the perceived problems in maintaining the application system vary according to the allocation of the maintenance effort. Correlation analysis indicates that, in general, problems are perceived to be the greater, the more relative time is spent in corrective maintenance. Of the twelve correlation coefficients relating the six problems to relative time spent in emergency fixes and routine debugging, eleven were positive, of which nine were statistically significant and five were notable. Relative time in emergency fixes was positively associated with problems of product quality (r = 0.200, s = 0.001); user knowledge (r = 0.130, s = 0.002); and programmer effectiveness (r = 0.117, s = 0.005). Relative time in routine debugging was positively associated with product quality (r = 0.204, s = 0.001) and programmer effectiveness (r = 0.132, s = 0.002). These findings are placed in good perspective when it is recalled that increased relative time in routine debugging was found earlier to be positively associated with the magnitude of the effort in maintenance. It is possible that management's assessment of the problems in maintenance reflects some intuitive appreciation of this consequence.

Two other relationships involving the allocation of the maintenance effort with problem factors were of notable significance and magnitude. The problem of machine requirements was positively associated with both recoding for computational efficiency (r = 0.164, s = 0.001) and accommodating system hardware and software changes (r = 0.106, s = 0.010). Both these relationships are easily understood.

Interestingly, no notable findings related the percent time spent in providing user enhancements to any of the problems of maintenance, including that of user knowledge. As might therefore be expected, a correlation analysis of the allocation of the enhancement effort and the problems of maintenance also produced no notable findings.

It is recalled from earlier discussions that the five general variables thus far related to the problems of maintenance--system size, system age, relative development experience, magnitude of maintenance effort, and allocation of maintenance effort--are themselves closely interrelated (see Figure 5.8). This suggests that the impact of these variables upon the problems of maintenance should be considered jointly. Based upon the causal structure suggested in Figure 5.8, a series of multiple regression analyses were thus performed, with the independent variables introduced hierarchically. Two measures of the magnitude of the maintenance effort were introduced first, followed by the two component measures of corrective maintenance, the five measures of system size, the single measure of relative development experience, and, lastly, system age. At each level of the hierarchy, measures were introduced according to their statistical significance at that step. (See Nie et al., (1975), for a discussion of the analytical procedure.) A summary of the results of the regression analyses is presented in Figure 7.8.

It is seen in Figure 7.8 that the magnitude of the effort in maintenance, the allocation of this effort to corrective maintenance, and relative development experience are all of importance in explaining the problems of maintenance. In particular, number of maintenance person-hours accounts for a substantial portion of the problem of programmer effectiveness, and the relative development experience of the maintainers and the percent time on corrective maintenance (which includes both emergency fixes and routine debugging) are of similar significance in accounting for the problem of product quality. These particular relationships offer ready interpretations. The problem of programmer effectiveness would tend to be recognized in those situations where much effort is being spent, on the one hand, and more effort would be required where this problem exists, on the other. Where the developers of a system also maintain it, complaints from these individuals about the quality of the developed product would presumably be minimized for psychological reasons, making this problem less visible on the whole. At the same time, less time is spent in corrective maintenance, presumably because of knowledge based in development experience, and this too would tend to dampen recognition of problems with product quality.

It may also be concluded from Figure 7.8 that system size and age have little influence upon the problems of maintenance, apart from their established impact upon the magnitude and allocation of the maintenance

Figure 7.8

Summary of Regression Analyses of Maintenance Problem Factors
With Measures of the Magnitude and Allocation
of the Maintenance Effort, System Size, and Development Experience

Problem Factor (Multiple R) Significant Independent Variables	RSQ Change	Beta
User knowledge (0.266)		
Maintenance person-hours	0.020	0.130
Percent emergency fixes	0.016	0.111
Development experience	0.018	-0.137
Programmer effectiveness (0.449)		
Maintenance person-hours	0.116	0.253
Percent emergency fixes	0.018	0.097
Number of files	0.012	0.134
Development experience	0.032	-0.162
Product quality (0.476)		
Maintenance person-hours	0.053	0.206
Percent emergency fixes	0.043	0.168
Percent routine debugging	0.021	0.137
Development experience	0.086	-0.280
Programmer time availability (0.213)		
Maintenance person-hours	0.019	0.094
Development experience	0.011	-0.118
Machine requirements (0.269)		
Number of files	0.026	0.200
Number of reports	0.022	-0.207
System reliability (0.312)		
Maintenance person-hours	0.027	0.124
Percent emergency fixes	0.019	0.133
Number of files	0.010	0.152
Number of programs	0.015	-0.167

effort, and the relative development experience of the maintainers. When the latter variables have been entered first into the regression equations, measures of system size have notable influence only upon the problems of machine requirements and system reliability, which together account for only 11.1% of the total problem variance. System age has no notable influence whatsoever.

The results of the present analysis may be generally summarized in Figure 7.9, which extends the causal synthesis of Figure 5.8. The new dependent variable of interest, the problems of maintenance, is shown to be directly influenced by three of the five variables earlier interrelated. The causal direction should be interpreted as follows: the problems of maintenance constitute a subjective valuation made, given the facts of relative development experience, relative amount of corrective maintenance, and the magnitude of the maintenance effort as a whole.

Analyses of variance of the six problem factors according to the use of system development tools were next performed. The results are summarized in Figure 7.10. The variance of the problem factor, product quality, according to the use of five of the eight tools is especially noteworthy. The software product is perceived to be of better quality (in terms of the three components from which the factor is derived: system design specifications, programming, and documentation) where test data generators, structured programming, HIPO, structured walk-through, or the chief programming team have been employed. These results should be heartening to advances of these techniques. However, it is also noteworthy that the problems of user knowledge and programmer effectiveness, which account together for 71.4% of the problem variance, are little effected through the use of these same techniques. Only structured programming is found associated with the problem of user knowledge, a result which offers no apparent interpretation, and no technique is associated with programmer effectiveness.

Greater problems of system reliability are seen to be associated with the use of a data base dictionary, reflecting perhaps the complexity of the system software which incorporates this tool. The problems of programmer time availability and machine requirements prove to be unrelated to the use of the development tools listed.

Figure 7.9

Some Relationships Involving the Problems of Maintenance

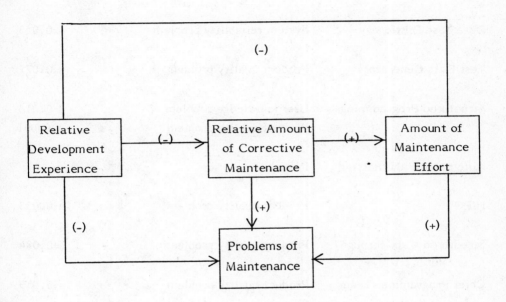

Figure 7.10

Analyses of Variance of Problems in Maintenance
By Use of Development Tools

Tools	Significantly Related Problem Factors	
Decision Tables	(None)	
Data Base Dictionary	System reliability problem	s=0.053
Test Data Generators	Product quality problem	s=0.077
Structured Programming	User knowledge problem	s=0.013
	Product quality problem	s 0.001
Automated Flowcharting	(None)	
HIPO	Product quality problem	s=0.033
Structured Walk-through	Product quality problem	s=0.084
Chief Programmer Team	Product quality problem	s=0.049

Analyses of variance of the six problem factors according to the use of a data base management system (DBMS) were also performed. No significant variances were found, and it may be concluded that management's assessment of the problems in maintenance is likely to be the same, on average, for application systems supported by a DBMS, as for application systems unsupported.

Also examined were the variances in the six maintenance problem factors according to the programming language used. The choice of programming language in application programming has long been a controversial issue, and it is frequently argued that one or another language is superior for maintenance purposes (see, for example, Rose (1978), who argues against the use of assembler languages, on this ground).

Employing a one-way analysis of variance, two problem factors were seen to vary significantly according to programming language used: programmer effectiveness (s = 0.010) and system reliability (s = 0.080). In the case of programmer effectiveness, problems tend to be slightly greater than average where assembler languages are used, and notably greater than average where FORTRAN or PL/1 is used. Where COBOL is used, problems of programmer effectiveness are about average, and where RPG is used, notably less than average. On the whole, it first appears, the more "sophisticated" the language, the greater are the problems in programmer effectiveness.

However, the interpretation of a direct causal relationship between programming language and the problem of programmer effectiveness proves not to be warranted. Other analyses suggest that the scale of the data processing environment may account for a portion of the relationship, since more sophisticated languages tend to be used in the larger environments, and the problems of programmer effectiveness tend also to be greater, the larger the organization (see page 148). To explore this possibility further, a two-way analysis of variance of the programmer effectiveness problem was conducted, controlling for the size of the data processing equipment budget, in addition to the programming language used. (A hierarchichal approach to the partitioning of main effects was employed, assigning priority to size of the data processing equipment budget, assumed to have causal precedence. See Nie et al., 1975.)

Results are presented in Figure 7.11. It is seen that the main effects of programming language are not significant at the $s \leq 0.100$ level, when the size of the equipment budget is controlled. Thus, the apparent relationship between programming language and the problem of programmer effectiveness is explained in terms of the data processing environment in which programming takes place. It may be that larger installations are characterized by more complex applications, for which more sophisticated languages are suited, and which, at the same time, present greater challenges to effective programming. However, other explanations are also possible.

In the case of system reliability, one-way analysis of variance showed the problem to be greater than average where FORTRAN is used, and less than average where RPG is used. For the other languages the problem is about average. Since other analysis indicates the problem of system reliability does not vary significantly with the size of the data processing equipment budget (see p. 148), the present apparent relationship may not be explained as with programmer effectiveness. Any interpretation here is tenuous, but it may be that RPG software is seen as more reliable, on the average, for applications programming, and FORTRAN is seen as less reliable. Alternatively, it may be that the relatively greater age of the FORTRAN based systems accounts for the problem of reliability.

The use of organizational controls was next investigated, in terms of its relationship to the problems of maintenance. Simple analyses of variance of the six problem factors were first performed. A total of 16 relationships were established at significance levels ranging from $s < 0.001$ to $s = 0.070$. Of these, 13 relationships were positive, suggesting that, on the whole, the use of organizational controls is associated with relatively greater problems in maintenance.

Noteworthy among the relationships established were associations with the use of three types of logs: the user request log, the operations trouble log, and the program change log. Nine associations with maintenance problems existed in these cases, and all were positive. Thus, the use of logs is strongly related to the extent of problems in maintenance.

Figure 7.11a

Analysis of Variance

Programmer Effectiveness Problem by Annual DP Budget and Principal Programming Language

Source of Variation	Sum of Squares	DF	Mean Square	F	Significance of F
Main effects	21.440	11	1.949	3.300	0.000
DP Budget	18.479	6	3.080	5.215	0.000
Prog. Language	2.961	5	0.592	1.003	0.416
Two-Way Interactions	19.809	23	0.861	1.458	0.080
DP Budget, Prog. Language	19.809	23	0.861	1.458	0.080
Explained	41.248	34	1.213	2.054	0.001
Residual	244.485	414	0.591		
Total	285.734	448	0.638		

487   cases were processed.
38   cases (7.8 percent) were missing.

Figure 7.11b

Multiple Classification Analysis

Programmer Effectiveness Problem by Annual DP Budget and Principal Programming Language

Variance and Category	N	Unadjusted Dev'n	Eta	Adjusted for Independents Dev'n	Beta
DP Budget					
Less than $125th	128	-0.26		-0.24	
$125th - 250th	77	-0.10		-0.09	
$250th - 500th	69	0.06		0.07	
$500th - 1 Mil	68	0.22		0.20	
$1 - 2 Mil	47	0.15		0.13	
$2 - 4 Mil	25	0.14		0.12	
$4 Mil or more	35	0.33	0.25	0.29	0.23
Programming Language					
COBOL	246	0.05		-0.01	
ASSEMBLER	49	0.14		0.09	
PL/1	17	0.30		0.14	
RPG	102	-0.24		-0.09	
FORTRAN	7	0.33		0.48	
Other	28	-0.06	0.18	0.00	0.10

Multiple R Squared 0.075
Multiple R Squared 0.274

However, no causal inferences should be made as yet from this analysis. Clearly, the intent in applying organizational controls must be to alleviate problems in maintenance, not to exacerbate them. Prior analysis has shown these problems to be associated with the magnitude and allocation of the maintenance effort, and the relative development experience of the maintainers (Figure 7.8). It was thus decided to further explore the impact of organizational controls upon maintenance problems, controlling for the influence of the previously established relationships.

A series of regression analyses were performed, with hierarchic entry of the independent variables. Entered first were the number of annual maintenance person-hours, the relative allocation of effort to emergency fixes and routine debugging, and the relative development experience of the maintainers. Organizational controls were then permitted to enter the equations. Results are summarized in Figure 7.12. It is seen that few associations between the problems of maintenance and the use of organizational controls exist, when the control variables have been accounted for. Of the associations which do exist, none are positive.

The periodic audit is shown in Figure 7.12 to contribute to a reduction in both problems of user knowledge and product quality. Previous analysis has shown the use of this control to be unrelated to the magnitude of the effort in maintenance, but related to the allocation of this effort in terms of spending relatively more time in providing user enhancements and less in emergency fixes. Spending relatively less time in emergency fixes is itself associated with lesser problems in maintenance. On the whole, then, the evidence is encouraging with respect to the use of the periodic audit in support of maintenance.

This completes the analysis of relationships involving the problem factors in maintenance with other application system variables determined through Part II of the questionnaire. In a final series of analyses, the problem factors are analyzed for possible relationships with the organizational variables of Part I.

Figure 7.12

Summary of Regression Analyses of Maintenance Problem Factors
With Use of Organizational Controls
Controlling for Magnitude and Allocation of Maintenance Effort
and Relative Development Experience

Problem Factor (Multiple R) Significant Controls	RSQ Change	Beta
User knowledge (0.308)		
Perodic audit	0.028	-0.162
Programmer effectiveness (0.362)		
(None)		
Product quality (0.491)		
Perodic audit	0.028	-0.165
Equipment cost charge-back	0.016	-0.170
Programmer time availability (0.279)		
Program change retest procedure	0.013	-0.091
User request justification	0.011	-0.095
Machine requirements (0.196)	None	
System reliability (0.245)	None	

Analyses of variance of the six problem factors according to the size of the data processing equipment budget were first performed. The results were quite striking. The variance of the factor, programmer effectiveness, was highly significant, at the $s < 0.001$ level, with linearity also significant at the $s \leq 0.001$ level, indicating the problem was perceived to be the greater, the larger the installation. No significant variances in the other five problem factors, including "machine requirements" and "system reliability," were found. Thus, the perceived problems of maintenance vary by the size of the organization along the single dimension of "programmer effectiveness." Two interpretations are suggested for consideration. The straightforward interpretation is that smaller organizations do have greater programmer effectiveness, possibly because the advantages of simplicity of work coordination outweigh the disadvantages of lack of technical specialization. An alternative interpretation is that programmer effectiveness does not itself vary, but that awareness of the "problem" is heightened according to the visibility of the data processing budget. Other interpretations may also be possible.

Variance in the six problem factors according to whether maintenance is separately organized was next analyzed. No significant variances were found. Thus, although less relative time is spent on maintenance by organizations which organize it separately (see Chapter 3), management's assessment of the problems does not differ. This is somewhat surprising, since it might reasonably be thought that managers would perceive their programmers as more effective, or programmer time as more available.

Maintenance problem factors were also correlated to the percent time spent on maintenance in the organization as a whole (Item 1.5 of the questionnaire). As might be expected, problems are seen to be the more severe, the more the organization's time is allocated to maintenance. Four of the six problem factors, accounting together for 88.9% of the problem variance, are of notable significance and magnitude: programmer effectiveness ($r = 0.191$, $s = 0.001$); product quality ($r = 0.158$, $s = 0.001$); user knowledge ($r = 0.113$, $s = 0.006$); and programmer time availability ($r = 0.101$, $s = 0.013$). System reliability is also positively related, though the magnitude is not notable. The problem of machine requirements is unrelated.

Finally, analyses of variance of the six problem factors by the perceived level of staffing sufficiency and the demands of maintenance on the manager's own time were performed. It was found that four problem factors varied significantly by perceived level of staffing sufficiency: user knowledge ($s = 0.007$); programmer effectiveness ($s < 0.001$); product quality ($s < 0.001$); and programmer time availability ($s < 0.001$). In each case, linearity was also significant at the $s = 0.003$ level or better, and it may be concluded that each problem tends to be perceived as greater, as the staffing level is regarded as less sufficient, on the whole. These are strong results, though not particularly surprising.

In the case of the demands of maintenance on the manager's own time, four problem factors also varied significantly: user knowledge ($s = 0.005$); programmer effectiveness ($s = 0.055$); product quality ($s < 0.001$); and system reliability ($s = 0.076$). Again, linearity was also significant in each case, here at the $s = 0.016$ level or better, and it may be concluded that each problem tends to be perceived as greater, the more of the manager's own time is absorbed by the demands of maintenance. As before, these results are what might be expected.

This completes the analysis of relationships associated with the problems of maintenance. In the next, final chapter, the results of the survey are summarized and conclusions are drawn.

148

CHAPTER EIGHT Conclusion

This chapter summarizes the results of the survey in terms of the issues identified in Chapter 1. Further, suggestions for future research are given, as are recommendations for data processing management. In doing this, it is necessary to depart from the more narrow inferential processes of the preceding chapters. In considering our conclusions, the reader is thus asked to weigh carefully the evidence and arguments offered here, in conjunction with those of his or her own experience and judgement.

It should further be noted that the suggestions for research and recommendations for management are closely related. Several of the research suggestions require the cooperation of management in order to be implemented. Similarly, certain of the recommendations for management involve experimentation, in which researchers may provide assistance. On the whole, close cooperation between researchers and management should prove fruitful.

A final section of this chapter seeks to place the research results in a wider context, both in terms of software of nontraditional types, and of a scenario for the possible future.

8.1   The Issues Revisited

What do the results of the survey indicate with respect to the five groups of issues which have been raised in the literature (discussed on pages 1.3-1.7)? What new issues may be identified, in addition? In this section, some answers to these questions are ventured.

Conceptual Issues

The fundamental question remains: What shall be meant by the term "maintenance?" In the present survey, respondents were asked to take an inclusive view. Specifically, the Introduction to the questionnaire indicated: "As used here, the term 'maintenance' refers to all modifications made to an existing application system, including enhancements and extensions." (See Appendix I.) This provisional definition sought to insure that all work on an existing application system would be reported, regardless of the local definition of maintenance.

What is the nature of the work performed on existing application systems? Here the results of the survey are clear. The work on existing application systems consists largely of continued development. (This conclusion agrees with that of Carlson, 1979.) The principal single activity is providing enhancements for users. (See Figure 5.2.)

Without necessarily quarreling with the above conclusion, other writers argue nevertheless for an exclusive view of the term "maintenance." They prefer to exclude enhancements and extensions from the concept. An inclusive view is considered "harmful," and the software engineer is encouraged to think of software as an engineer thinks of a bridge:

> The software engineer should see the analogy: repairing of a bridge may be routine maintenance, but adding a third lane to a two-lane bridge - the highway engineer does not call it "maintenance!" Equally important, he does not think of it as "maintenance." (Jones, 1978)

Evidently, the harmfulness of the inclusive view arises when enhancements and extensions are carried out routinely, (e.g., without a cost-benefit justification). In this, there may be some truth, though the problem should not occur if all maintenance is, on the whole, justified in terms of continuing cost-benefit assessments. (See the recommendation for life cycle audits in Section 8.3)

But is software really comparable to a bridge? It does not deteriorate physically (Brooks, 1975), so the repairing analogy fails. On the other hand, it may "deteriorate" logically, in terms of structural integrity, with severe consequences, as Winograd (1979) has described:

> Using current programming techniques, systems often reach a point at which the accretion of changes makes their structure so baroque and opaque that further changes are impossible, and the performance of the system is irreversibly degraded. (p.392)

While the structural integrity of a bridge may also be compromised (one thinks of the proposal to double-deck the Golden Gate Bridge in San Francisco, for example), it is not clear that this is a sufficient basis to support the analogy.

A more serious problem with the bridge analogy is that the practical use of application software has, to date, typically required that a "new lane" be added for each additional user. Enhancements and extensions have not been a sometime event! The manager who would treat them as such would thus not be responsible to the users of the system.

Fortunately, the advent of data base management systems, together with generalized inquiry capability, may alleviate this serious problem. By means of this technology, it may be increasingly possible to "export" much current enhancement work to the user groups themselves. (See the recommendations in Section 8.3)

In our view, the basic conceptual issue is not the definition of "maintenance" per se, but rather the development of a theoretically sound and practically useful classification system for all work performed on existing application systems. The categories of classification should be mutually exclusive and exhaustive, in so far as possible, as well as economical and significant. The classification system suggested by Swanson (1976) is a first step in this direction. It has been shown in the results of this survey to be theoretically useful. Further, it has been adapted for use by at least one government agency. However, it is by no means definitive, and further development and refinement is warranted. (See Section 8.2)

Scale-of-Effort Issues

What is the relative amount of organizational resources typically allocated to application system maintenance? Is there a trend toward an increase in this amount? Do older systems require increased maintenance? These are the scale-of-effort questions which have dominated the literature. As was seen in Chapter 1, a number of estimates have been made in answer to these questions. However, these have been based on rather limited data. The present survey provides a more substantial basis for the making of estimates.

Results of the survey indicate that about half the time of applications systems and programming staff is spent on maintenance in the average department. This estimate is consistent with the middle range of estimates given in the literature. Larger data processing organizations do tend to spend relatively more time on maintenance than smaller departments, but the mean percentage varies only from 44.4% to 53.5% across all equipment budget categories. Thus, estimates of 70% or more, while certainly applicable to some organizations, are not representative of data processing organizations as a whole.

Further, the assertion that the maintenance percentage is rapidly growing--which some contend--is not borne out by the survey. The average percentage has, in fact, apparently remained at about the same level over a two year period. (See Figure 3.5) On the other hand, results also suggest that the amount of maintenance performed on an individual existing system may tend to increase, rather than decrease, with time. (See pages 5.3-5.4.) Therefore, if an organization's inventory of existing systems were to grow and age continuously, only an indefinite growth in the overall staffing level would enable a constant percentage of resources to be allocated to new system development. Such an easy availability of resources is an unlikely explanation of a constant percentage allocation to maintenance.

How is the level of maintenance controlled by management? When the nature of maintenance is recalled, the obvious explanation is suggested. Maintenance consists in large part of continued development, much of which is no doubt discretionary. By "freezing" the continued development of an existing system, resources may be transferred to the development of a new replacement system. Such activity may be employed on a continuous basis to maintain a balance between maintenance and new system development.

Data processing management of application systems should probably be thought of in portfolio terms. Existing systems provide the current benefits, but often at increasing costs with age. New systems provide new or additional future benefits, or reductions in costs. Uncertainty about the future poses cost-benefit risks for both existing and new systems. With limited resources, management must make difficult choices in its allocation of effort between maintenance and new system development. Current and future benefits and costs, together with associated risks, must be balanced within the application system portfolio. (See further discussion under Section 8.2)

Organizational Issues

One of the foremost issues in the literature has been the overall organization of the maintenance effort. Canning (1972) and Mooney (1975) support the concept of a separate maintenance group. The benefits perceived include the control of effort and costs. The analysis here offers some support for this contention. Departments where maintenance is organized separately from new system development tend to spend relatively less time on maintenance. (See page 16.)

However, an additional finding poses something of a dilemma. In the maintenance of individual application systems, experience of maintenance personnel in the development of the system correlates significantly with less effort in maintenance. (See pages 68-70.) Unfortunately, organizing separately while keeping system staff intact would result in continuous migration into maintenance. (Mills, 1976)

Should development experience be sacrificed in organizing separately? In Section 8.3, we suggest that the concept of a maintenance escort, to accompany a system transferred from new development, be explored by data processing management.

What organization controls are effective in maintenance? Here, the survey findings are very limited. Four controls, three of which are logging and documenting procedures, were used in more than half the systems described. Little evidence was found to indicate that these or other controls had any substantial impact upon the level of effort in maintenance. In terms of the allocation of the maintenance effort, the use of a control sometimes proved symptomatic of the problem to which it was presumably addressed. For example, there was a tendency to log and document user requests where a relatively greater effort was spent in providing user enhancements. Only in the case of the periodic audit were the results particularly interesting. Here, it was found that use of the audit was associated with relatively less time spent on emergency fixes, and more on providing user enhancements, a desirable trade-off. (See the recommendation for life cycle audits in Section 8.3)

Productivity Technique Issues

As was indicated in Chapter 1, productivity techniques have been much discussed, but little studied, in the literature.

How widely are productivity techniques used? The present survey indicates that only decision tables, structured programming, and the chief programmer team were used in the development of 20% or more of the systems studied. (See Figure 4.9) This observation is conditioned on the respondents interpretation of the terms. Other aids were not widely used. This may be explained, in part, by the age distribution of the systems surveyed. The median age was 3 years, 4 months, and a significant few (32, 6.6%) were over 10 years old. (See Figure 4.2) Thus, the development of the older systems precedes the appearance and marketing of the newer productivity techniques.

Larger organizations made significantly greater use of productivity techniques, on the whole. They also have more resouces to introduce new techniques. However, no significant general trend toward increased use of the techniques was detected.

In terms of impact, little evidence was found to support generalized claims of savings in maintenance personnel effort achieved through the use of productivity aids. However, there was an indication that the allocation of the maintenance effort was enhanced through the use of aids, in the sense of relatively greater attention given to adaptive and perfective maintenance, as opposed to corrective maintenance. This finding was corroborated by a related result, wherein management reported problems with software quality to be significantly less, in those cases where certain of the productivity aids were employed. Among the problems of maintenance, however, the factor "user knowledge" dominates all others. (See below.) This factor was found to be little affected by current productivity techniques. This suggests that the development of new techniques might be directed, in part, specifically to the user interface. (See the discussion in Section 8.2)

Problem Area Issues

Problems viewed as significant in the literature were not always seen in the same light by the respondents to the present survey. For example, motivation of maintenance programmers was one of the lowest ranking problem items. Neither was maintenance personnel turnover viewed as serious, compared to other problems. On the other hand, results confirm that documentation quality is one of the most important issues. Planning is also a problem, in terms of competing demands for maintenance personnel time and the meeting of scheduled commitments. (See Figures 5.6 and 5.19.)

The most important problem item proved to be user demands for enhancements and extensions, confirming the results of an earlier survey. (Lientz, et. al., 1978) Further, the factor "user knowledge" accounted for about 60% of the common (explained) problem variance. (See Figure 5.20.) The importance of the user relationship to maintenance is thus underscored.

Potential determinants of the problems in maintenance were also analyzed. Problems of programmer effectiveness and product quality were seen to be relatively greater for systems which were older and larger, and where more relative effort in corrective maintenance was spent. All problem factors were positively associated with the level of effort in maintenance. A tendency toward lesser problems in maintenance existed, where the maintenance programmers were also involved in the development of the system. The problem of product quality was seen as lesser, where certain productivity techniques were used in development. Among various organizational controls, only the periodic audit seemed usefully related, by means of its association with lesser problems of user knowledge and product quality. Larger scale data processing environments were significantly associated with greater problems of programmer effectiveness, but with no other problem factor.

8.2 Suggestions For Further Research

Heretofore, much research activity has been directed at improved programming techniques. Software engineering has been oriented in particular to improved design and construction. The results reported here do not negate this effort. Rather they emphasize that technical concerns focus on only one part of the problem. Overall, the analysis indicates that major concerns exist in the managerial and user related areas of software maintenance. These are areas where very little is being done. To illustrate, Merwin (1978), in a review of articles which had appeared to that recent date in the IEEE Transactions on Software Engineering, notes that only two were categorized as dealing with software management.

Our own suggestions for future research will thus be centered on the managerial and user-related areas. Included are suggestions for: (i) a theory of application system portfolio management; (ii) improved methods of information requirements assessment; (iii) user problem studies; (iv) user application development packages; (v) the design of management control systems; (vi) organizational design experiments; (vii) the study of system growth characteristics; (viii) longitudinal life cycle studies. Each of these will be discussed briefly, as space permits.

Application System Portfolio Management

A first suggestion is for the development of a "portfolio theory" of application system management. As discussed in the previous section, management must allocate its resources between new system development and maintenance, among systems both old and new. Systems are originated, developed, implemented, maintained, and replaced or terminated. The survey evidence is that management seeks to achieve a balance in the overall allocation process, between new system development and maintenance.

But a theory of how the balance ought to be struck is lacking. Research in this direction is thus a priority concern.

A portfolio theory of application system management would focus attention not only on the acquisition of new systems, but on the disposal of old ones, a wholly neglected subject. Decision models for deciding on whether to terminate an existing system, in whole or in part, would be included. A theory of system replacement should also emerge from this perspective.

Information Requirements Assessment

A second suggestion is for the development of better methods of information requirements assessment. As has been seen, user demands for enhancements and extensions is the major problem in maintenance. Determining information requirements is the process of interpreting and evaluating these demands. All subsequent maintenance activities hinge upon the results of this process. For this reason, information requirements assessment is a subject of major importance.

While various tools and techniques have been proposed in support of information requirements assessment, an integrative theory is generally lacking. (Cooper and Swanson, 1979) Further research is much needed.

The current orientation in information requirements assessment is toward "getting the requirements right." (Canning, 1977) This orientation is motivated by the desire to avoid unnecessary redesign and reprogramming in later stages of the system life cycle. However, it may be based upon a fallacious assumption, viz. that requirements may be "fixed" for practical design and implementation purposes. The reality seems to be that the notion of what is "required" changes continuously, often in response to organizational change. Changes in organizational expectations are particularly significant in this regard, and such changes are more likely to be influenced by experience in using an information system, than by abstract specification of needs in early phases of the design process. The major problem in requirements assessment

159

may not be a complete, consistent, and unambiguous specification, prior to design, as currently emphasized. (See, e.g., Teichroew and Hershey, 1977.) Rather the problem may be timely and sensitive response to organizational change, over the full life cycle. Requirements assessment in maintenance may thus be a problem fully as demanding as in new system development.

Surveys of the current literature in information requirements assessment include Taggart and Tharp (1977), Bariff (1977), and Cooper and Swanson (1979).

User Problem Studies

A third suggestion is for user problem studies - studies of application systems problems as assessed by users, as opposed to data processing management.

From the viewpoint of data processing management, user demand for enhancements and extensions is the most significant of problems in maintenance, and the factor "user knowledge" accounts for a substantial proportion of the common problem variance. But would users see things in the same way?

One useful research approach would be to study the problems of ongoing systems from the viewpoints of users, as opposed to data processing professionals. Problem factors, from the user's perspective, might be identified and correlated to the corresponding problem factors, as seen by data processing management. An interesting question is whether the user knowledge problem factor would be recognized by the users themselves. If not, how would the users see the problem? Further, what characteristics of user environments would explain the variance in their problem perceptions?

By approaching the "user problem" from both sides, a more enlightened understanding of the problems of application software maintenance should ultimately be expected.

User Application Development Packages

It would seem also worthwhile to provide users with tools with which to develop their own application systems, insofar as possible. A substantial portion of the maintenance burden might thereby be assumed by the organizational units which are the ultimate beneficiaries of the application systems. The decision to bear a maintenance burden could then be effectively decentralized.

Thus, another research suggestion is directed toward user application development packages - sets of tools which support users in application system development. Of major importance among these tools would be user-oriented languages, (e.g., Query-by Example (QBE)), which enable users to interact with an established data base. (Zloof, 1977.) Also important would be directories, and documentation support systems.

A wholly reasonable objective for these development packages would be the limited enhancement and extension of systems already installed. A more ambitious objective would be the development of new systems.

In recent months, the concepts of the "programmer's workbench" (Dolotta and Mashey, 1976) and the "analyst's workbench" (Canning, 1979) have been advanced to support application system development by programmers and analysts. Extending these concepts, a "user's workbench" might also be considered. Its major purpose might be to enable a user to further develop an existing application system, within some controlled framework.

Applications most suitable for development by users, as opposed to data processing professionals, are those whose scope is limited to the computing needs of the individual person or department. (McLean, 1979) This segment of the application system population may be expected to grow in direct proportion to the availability of tools to support development by users.

The design of user application development packages should be guided, in part, by user problem studies such as those recommended above.

Management Control Systems

Research directed at the design of management control systems for maintenance is also suggested. Several of the more frequently cited problems in maintenance, including competing demands for programmer time and meeting scheduled commitments, indicate that the allocation of resources in maintenance requires enhanced support.

Among the problems to be addressed in managment control are: the measurement and monitoring of the maintenance process; the design of systems for receiving and recording user demands; the forecast and management of future user demands; work allocation strategies and tactics; transfer pricing systems for products and services; maintenance cost estimation techniques; user responsibilities and roles in maintenance; and application system auditing.

Some general guidelines for the design of a management control system in maintenance are given by Fink (1977), who emphasizes the need for flexibility in adapting to change.

Inasmuch as the design of management control systems is not a problem original to data processing management, researchers should pay particular attention to design lessons learned in other service-related areas of application, (e.g., consulting and social services administration).

Organizational Design Experiments

Experiments in organizational designs for maintenance are also recommended. As has been seen, research results indicate that a unitary maintenance organization may be associated with enhanced productivity in maintenance. However, the evidence is only fragmentary and suggestive; it is not the product of controlled experimentation. Similarly, results suggest that productivity gains may be achieved where systems are maintained by the same individuals who developed them. Here again, experimentation is needed to provide more solid evidence.

Fully controlled experimentation in field studies, as opposed to laboratory research, is typically not possible. But "quasi-experimental" designs may be achieved. Designs which should be considered in the current context include the nonequivalent control group, the separate-sample pretest-post-test, and the multiple time series. (Campbell and Stanley, 1966) Each of these offers decided advantages over the pre-experimental designs more frequently encountered: the one-shot case study, the one-group pretest-post-test, and the static-group comparison.

System Growth Characteristics

More detailed studies of the growth characteristics of application software are also needed. The evidence here is that application systems grow with age, but at a declining rate. However, the present study is based solely on "snapshots" of currently maintained systems, at varying single points in the respective system life cycles. Needed are longitudinal studies which track system growth at multiple points over a significant time horizon. (Exemplary of that which is needed is the work of Belady and Lehman, 1976.)

What is the pattern of system growth over the full life cycle? A reasonable conjecture is that it approximates the logistic curve in form. (See Figure 8.1) In development, system growth begins slowly, with the initial programs requiring much definitional support. Learning curve effects are also noticeable. With basic parameters in place, and familiarity acquired, the rate of code production increases to some maximum level, before constraints in objectives and resources force a natural decline. At some point in this later phase, with the application system still growing at a significant rate, installation takes place. Growth continues at a declining rate after installation.

The logistic curve is a general system growth curve, which has many counterparts in nature, where resources for growth are limited. (Bertalanffy, 1968) In data processing, it has also been applied to the growth of data processing organizations. (Nolan, 1973)

Figure 8.1

The Pattern of Application System Growth

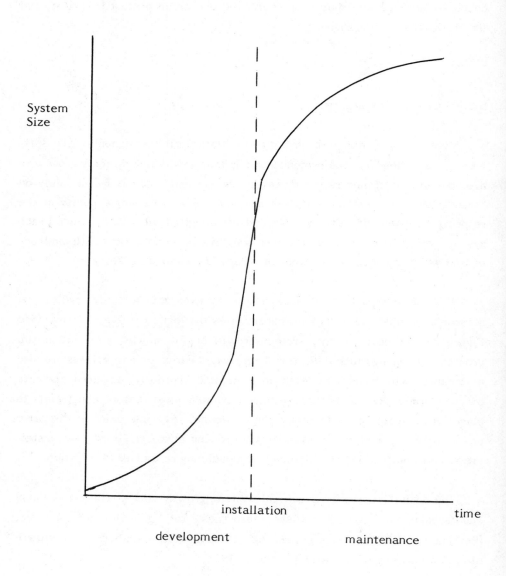

Longitudinal Life Cycle Studies

Longitudinal studies are needed, not only of system growth, but of the maintenance process itself. Research results here indicate that the allocation of maintenance may vary with system age, with older systems requiring relatively greater corrective maintenance. However, additional study is required to confirm and assess this finding. To what extent does it reflect a decline in the structural integrity of systems with age? To what extent does it too reflect declining familiarity with the system due to personnel reassignments and turnover? Further, are newer programming techniques, such as structured programming, likely to alleviate the current tendency?

To answer questions such as those just raised, it will be in part necessary to monitor system change over a significant portion of the life cycle.

Life cycle studies of changes in the problem perceptions associated with the maintenance of an application system may also be useful in diagnosing the effects of system age.

On the basis of the research reported here, what recommendations for the management of maintenance might be suggested? In the paragraphs to follow, we address this question.

In considering the recommendations which follow, the reader is cautioned that these apply to data processing departments of the general type surveyed. On the whole, this type is characterized by: (i) an orientation to traditional business and administrative data processing; (ii) responsibility for both development and maintenance of systems for internal organizational use; (iii) a captive market for products and services.

The recommendations are for: (i) the adoption of a system maintenance perspective; (ii) the use of life cycle audits; (iii) growth management; (iv) the monitoring of maintenance; (v) the adoption of user-based performance speci- fications; (vi) the export of user access to the system; (vii) the establishment of a user development program; (viii) the use of a unitary maintenance organization; and (ix) the use of maintenance escorts. Each of these will be discussed briefly, as space permits.

The System Maintenance Perspective

A first suggestion is the adoption of a system maintenance, as opposed to a program maintenance, perspective. The traditional program-centered per- spective sees the software as that which must be maintained. In the extreme, it is the individual program which is the unit of maintenance, from this narrow point of view. In contrast, a system-centered perspective regards the entire application system as the unit of maintenance. Software is treated not as individual programs, but rather as an integrated family. Further, the software is only one component of the system. Other components may include: user guides, operating instructions, standards and procedures, test procedures and data, project documentation, operating schedules, budgets, personnel and equipment plans, accounting statements, user profiles, utilization evaluations, a data base dictionary and directory, forms and report registers, volume logs, and a thesaurus, among others. (Swanson, 1979) These multiple components, all of which take the form of documents, may be usefully organized into libraries, (e.g., suggested by Cave and Salisbury (1978)).

The system maintenance perspective recognizes that a properly functioning application system is the product of an integrated socio-technical process, one involving people as well as computer and communications technology. The need for this perspective is underscored by the survey findings on the problems of maintenance. Problems with users, as opposed to software, predominate. Management problems in allocating scarce resources are also noteworthy. Problems with documentation quality tend too to be relatively important. Most, if not all of these problems should be alleviated, in our judgement, through the adoption of a system maintenance perspective.

One implication of the system-centered perspective is that a system analyst, as opposed to a programmer, should have primary responsibility for maintenance of an application system.

Life Cycle Audits

Audits of existing application systems are one of the lesser used organizational controls. Only one application system in three, among those surveyed, was subjected to a formal, periodic audit. However, the use of a periodic audit proved to be significantly associated with an enhanced allocation of the maintenance effort. Thus, it is recommended here for more widespread adoption.

In particular, it is recommended that audits be conducted over the full system life cycle. Audits during early phases of development may identify various problems, (e.g., design compromises and schedule slippages, which may occasionally warrant terminating a project to cut one's losses). An implementation audit may be used to confirm the installation of an application system, and to transfer it to maintenance responsibility. Subsequent audits may monitor the integrity of the system, assess the extent to which it meets the needs of its users, and determine its ultimate retirement and/or replacement.

Current practice in application system auditing often emphasizes the earlier phases of the life cycle. For example, Perry and FitzGerald (1977) describe 15 life cycle control points used in one government organization for auditing; none of these control points is concerned with operation and maintenance. Such neglect is not warranted. Substantial costs of operation and maintenance must typically be borne, over a time period exceeding that of all previous phases combined, where further development of the system is continuous. Auditing resources should be allocated accordingly.

In conducting the life cycle audits, particular attention should be paid to the system maintenance perspective mentioned above.

Also, inasmuch as audits represent an overhead cost to be borne, the total resources allocated to this activity should be commensurate with the scale of the application systems being maintained.

Growth Management

A third recommendation applies to the growth of both the data processing department and the collection of application systems maintained. Two major sources of growth may be identified. The first is a corresponding growth in the size and diversity/complexity of the organization served. The second is the pattern of development which follows computer acquisition, as described by Nolan (1973).

A substantial proportion of the data processing units surveyed here were of modest size; 29% had an annual equipment budget of less than $125,000. This proportion should hold steady, or even increase in the future, adjusting for inflation, as computing is made more cost-effective for the small organization. With more widespread adoption of computing, and the corresponding growth of many of these small organizations, the management of the growth of an application system portfolio should be recognized as a problem in its own right.

Growth management entails planning _for_ growth. As Nolan (1973) has characterized the typical pattern, proliferation of applications in the "contagion" stage precedes subsequent institution and integration of controls. Unnecessary difficulty in these later stages may be expected, if the preceding growth has not been orderly and well documented. For example, if management does not possess good data on application system size (see Figure 4.8), it may not be able to recognize and substantiate its maintenance burden.

It is thus recommended that the major growth phase of an application system portfolio be accompanied by the institution of a record keeping system which describes this portfolio in substantial detail.

The Monitoring of Maintenance

Just as the application system portfolio should be well documented, so too should the respective development and maintenance efforts. As has been seen (Figure 5.5), less than 40% of the organizations surveyed possess good data on personnel time allocated to maintenance. Somewhat over 40% possess minimal data, and almost 20% report no data whatsoever. This clearly provides little support for the management of the maintenance process.

At a minimum, each data processing organization should track the total hours allocated to the maintenance of each application system. Since this data collection also has implications for personnel assessment, care should be taken to insure the support of those reporting the basic data. Further, the precision sought should be only that needed. (Mason and Swanson, 1979) However, the standard of providing "good data" for management decision making should be met.

Most data processing organizations will also find a maintenance allocation classification system useful for management purposes. (Swanson, 1976) In particular, it should be useful to distinguish discretionary activities from those which are "unavoidable." The sensitivity with which this distinction is made may be extremely influential with respect to management's perception of its maintenance decision alternatives.

User-based Performance Specifications

A further recommendation is for the adoption of user-based performance specifications in application system development and maintenance. User-based performance specifications are defined here as those based on the performance of users and user organizations. Examples include the time required to process a customer order, the cost to maintain an inventory, and the market share to be achieved by a product or service. Such specifications have the fundamental virtue of identifying the organizational impact expected of a computer-based application system.

Narrowly conceived specifications, such as that of the content, format, and timing of a particular management report, are necessary but not sufficient for system development and maintenance. They are necessary because they define an output for a data processing task. They are not sufficient, however, because they say nothing about the responsiveness of this output to organizational information and decision making needs.

Among the findings of the present study is that user demands for enhancements and extensions constitutes the major problem for application system maintenance. These demands originate in the information and decision making needs of user organizations. It is thus appropriate that such needs be articulated in terms of performance specifications to be supported by the associated application systems. Insofar as possible, these specifications should be as "operational," (i.e., as well-defined) as the more narrowly conceived specifications.

User-based performance specifications provide a rationale for the existence of an application system. As such, they should serve as standards in support of the life cycle audits.

Export of User Access to System

As has been seen, application system maintenance consists largely of continued system development. Further, this development itself consists substantially of providing the user with additional reports, or new data in existing reports. (See Figure 5.3) In many situations, this may involve no more than an enhancement of user access to an already existing data base. Thus, one way to alleviate the maintenance burden may be to "export" this access from the data processing department to the user organizations themselves.

It may be that functional specifications for application systems should be of two distinct types:

-   Processing specifications--requirements for data collection, input, processing, storage and organization.

-   Reporting specifications--requirements for output data, reports, inquiry capability.

Maintenance of the system in terms of processing specifications would be the responsibility of the data processing department. Maintenance in terms of reporting specifications would be the responsibility of user organizations.

Under the proposed allocation of responsibilities, user demands for enhancements and extensions communicated to the data processing department would be limited to those with implications for processing specifications. A data base approach is implied, in that the basic functional output provided the user is a data base to which he or she has access.

Successful export of user access requires that user organizations become somewhat more sophisticated in their use of application systems. In particular, users may need to make use of terminal devices and/or report-generating languages in achieving the access desired. While some organizations have already moved in this direction, which is substantially that advocated by data base theorists and practitioners, many others have yet to follow. Less than 15% of the application systems surveyed here were supported by a data base management system.

The User Development Program

Another recommendation is for the establishment of user development programs, designed to increase user familiarity, knowledge, and sophistication in the use of application systems. Such programs should be directed toward alleviation of the "user knowledge" problem which has been identified in this research as being of fundamental importance.

Typically, the training of users is regarded as a task to be undertaken prior to implementation. As has been seen here, however, the problem of user knowledge is persistent among operational systems. In part, this may reflect deficiencies in pre-implementation practices. However, it is also likely that post-implementation change within the user organization, in particular, turn-over among personnel, creates situations which tend to undermine previously established familiarity and expertise. For this reason, user development programs should support application systems over their full life cycles.

User development programs should be a cooperative effort between the data processing department and user organizations. However, primary direction should be the responsibility of the user organizations.

Activities which might be undertaken as part of a user development program include: (i) the establishment of a standard classroom system familiarization package; (ii) the design and implementation of tutorial functions within the application system itself; (iii) job rotation and/or enlargement for selected users, to provide multiple-role experience with the application system.

One useful by-product of the user development program might be an enhanced articulation of demands for enhancements and extensions.

The Unitary Maintenance Organization

There is some evidence to suggest that a unitary maintenance organization, i.e. one which is distinct from that responsible for new system development, may lead to improved maintenance productivity. (See page 30). It is therefore proposed that such a unitary organization be considered for experimental adoption by data processing departments of size sufficient to support this functional division of labor.

The unitary maintenance organization may achieve certain of its productivity gains through individual expertise developed in maintenance specialization. Or, concentration of the maintenance task among relatively fewer persons may result in more efficient communication and cooperation. A third possibility is that maintenance may become more controllable in the unitary organization, because it is more visible. Which, if any, of these situations prevails in a given organization should be carefully studied by management, in the experimental formation of a unitary maintenance group. The effect of such an organization on new system development should also be closely monitored, to insure that productivity gains in one segment of the total effort are not achieved at the expense of productivity losses in the other.

The adoption of a unitary maintenance organization should be treated as an organizational design experiment. (See page 164). Management may thus wish to be advised by information system researchers, in conducting the experiment.

The Maintenance Escort

A final recommendation is for experimentation in the use of maintenance escorts, a term used here to refer to individuals who accompany a system transferred from development to maintenance responsibility. The maintenance escort is intended to provide for continuity in the further development of a system, in situations where maintenance and new system development are organized separately, and system turnover thus takes place upon installation.

As has been discussed, experience in development of a system contributes to productivity in its maintenance. (See Chapter 5). But with the unitary maintenance organization, this experience would be lost, unless some individual(s) moved with the system from the development unit to the maintenance unit.

The role of the maintenance escort would be a temporary one. As soon as the application system was judged to be efficiently absorbed within the maintenance unit, the escort would gradually be extricated from maintenance responsibility, and returned to the development unit for reassignment. Alternatively, should maintenance prove to be suited to the individual's skills and interests, the escort might remain in the maintenance unit in a more permanent assignment.

The concept of the maintenance escort has ample precedent in other organizational contexts. For example, engineers involved in new product development sometimes take temporary assignments in manufacturing, as initial production gets under way. Their experience with and commitment to the product can be of fundamental importance in insuring an efficient transition.

A variant of the maintenance escort role proposed here has been suggested by Cooper (1978). In this variant, the home base of the escort is in the maintenance unit; the individual participates in all phases of system development as a "representative" of the maintenance unit.

Because the maintenance escort is a specialized role, it is most appropriate for the large organizations, where such specialization can be most cost effective.

8.4   A Concluding Perspective

To conclude, we will attempt to place the results of the present research, as well as the conclusions and recommendations, in a broader perspective. The scope of the survey will first be reviewed, in terms of the types of organizations and software covered. Areas not covered will be commented upon. This will be followed by a look to the future. The prospective place of application software maintenance in the data processing organization of this future will be discussed.

A Word About Scope

This survey and the attendant analysis have focused on commercial data processing applications. These may be batch or on-line. They may exist in government or in industry. But they are primarily mainline production systems. The reason for this attention is obvious. This is the area where most maintenance expenditures occur.

Not included in the survey was maintenance of the hardware or system software underlying data processing applications. Maintenance of these products is obviously an important concern. However, it is not within the scope of the present research. The interest here has been with the more neglected subject of application software.

What else has been left out?   One area is esoteric military and communication systems. Examples are airborne command and control type systems. These are often programmed in assembly language. The environment of the software is harsh--hardware is changing and there are severe processing and memory requirements. This is obviously different from the data processing environments cited in the study. However, there are some similarities. User requests still must be managed. Work must be assessed. Productivity is still a key issue. For example, it has been estimated that increasing overall programmer productivity by just one instruction per man-day could save the

U.S. $45 million per year in defense system development and maintenance. (DeRoze and Nyman, 1978)

Another area is office automation. Office systems are somewhat different from traditional applications. However, the same types of controls are needed for text and electronic messages as for data to ensure integrity and security. Maintenance and integrity of archival applications will share many problems in common with data processing.

Related to office automation is the area of personal computing. The language APL is among those proposed for this area. At first blush there appears to be little need for organized maintenance. Yet consider the person without the computer. He or she collects and files algorithms, descriptions, drawings, etc., to be reused on later work--to save time. APL programmers often do the same. A subroutine library of utilities is thus built to facilitate future development. A need will exist to maintain and access these utilities.

In sum, many of the maintenance problems of traditional data processing are likely to apply to the newer forms of computer applications now appearing. Further, as the range of application widens, the total volume of developed software to be maintained will increase accordingly.

A Scenario of the Future

In conclusion, a scenario can be constructed for maintenance in the future. Assuming that managerial and technical tools are in place, the effort at corrective maintenance should ultimately be reduced. This will free some resources. Having users perform data entry and report retrievals will also reduce some of the simpler enhancement requests, thereby making available further resources. This is, however, the foreseeable limit. The remainder of the work is enhancement of a more substantial nature--changes in processing, using multiple files, etc. Some of this might be offloaded by the use of a data base management system. But there are limits here too.

The offloading of work and reduced routine work will make technical jobs more demanding. New productivity tools may be needed to assist in analysis, design, and programming.

In general, a decline and de-emphasis in maintenance and enhancement is not forseen. Rather the maintenance work of the future will be more complex and demanding. Measurement, control, and integrity become even more important since in our scenario users have direct access to the data base/files. Sophistication in accounting for usage will also have to increase.

However, fears that maintenance will completely dominate the world of the future are probably not warranted. Rather, management will learn to manage applications as a portfolio, and older systems will be retired and replaced on a regular basis, providing continuing opportunities for new system development.

REFERENCES

1. Ackoff, R.l. "Management Misinformation Systems". Management Science December, 1967, B147-B156.

2. Bariff, M.L. "Information Requirements Analysis: A Methodological Review". Working Paper #76-08-02. Decision Sciences Department, The Wharton School, University of Pennsylvania, December 1977.

3. Belady, L.A. and M.M. Lehman. "A Model of Large Program Development". IBM Systems Journal 3, 1976, 225-252.

4. Bertalanffy, L. General System Theory. New York: Braziller, 1968.

5. Boehm, B.W. "The High Cost of Software". Proceedings of Symposium on the High Cost of Software, Monterey, California, 1973, 27-40.

6. Boehm, B.W., J.R. Brown and M. Lipow. "Quantitative Evaluation of Software Quality". Proceedings, 2nd International Conference on Software Engineering, San Francisco, 13-15 October, 1976, 592-605.

7. Boehm, B.W. "Software Engineering". IEEE Transactions on Computers, C-25, December 1976, 1226-1241.

8. Brantley, C.L. and Y.R. Osajima. "Continuing Development of Centrally Developed and Maintained Software Systems". IEEE Computer Society Proceedings, 45, 1975, 285-288.

9. Brooks, F.P., Jr. The Mythical Man-Month, Reading, Mass.: Addison -Wesley, 1975.

10. Bucher, D.E.W. "Maintenance of the Computer Sciences Teleprocessing System". Proceedings, 1975 International Conference on Reliable Software, April 1975, 260-266.

11. Campbell, D.T. and J.C. Stanley. Experimental and Quasi-Experimental Designs for Research. Chicago: Rand McNally, 1969.

12. Canning, R.G. (ed.) "That Maintenance Iceberg". EDP Analyzer 10, 1972.

13. Canning, R.G. (ed.) "Getting the Requirements Right". EDP Analyzer, 15, July 1977.

14. Canning, R.G. (ed.) "The Analysis of User Needs". EDP Analyzer, 17, January 1979.

15. Carlson, E.D. "Trends in Application Development Languages". Computers & Information Systems Colloquium, Graduate School of Management, University of California, Los Angeles, March 8, 1979.

16. Cave, W.C. and A.B. Salisbury. "Controlling the Software Life Cycle - The Project Management Task". IEEE Transactions on Software Engineering, SE-4, July 1978, 326-334.

17. Champine, G.A. "What Makes a System Reliable?" Datamation, 24, September 1978, 195-206.

18. Cooper, J.D. "Corporate Level Software Management". IEEE Transactions on Software Engineering, SE-4, July 1978, 319-325.

19. Cooper, R.B. and E.B. Swanson. "Management Information Requirements Assessment: The State of the Art", and "Management Information Requirements Assessment: An Annotated Bibliography". Information Systems Working Papers 9-79 and 10-79. Graduate School of Management, University of California, Los Angeles, June 1979.

20. Daly, E.B. "Management of Software Development". IEEE Transactions on Software Engineering, SE-3, May 1977, 229-242.

21. DeRoze, B.C. and T.H. Nyman. "The Software Life Cycle - A Management and Technological Challenge in the Department of Defense". IEEE Transactions on Software Engineering, SE-4, July 1978, 309-318.

22. Ditri, A.E., J.C. Shaw, and W. Atkins. Managing the EDP Function. New York: McGraw-Hill, 1971.

23. Dolotta, T.A. and J.R. Mashey. "An Introduction to the Programmer's Workbench". Proceedings, 2nd International Conference on Software Engineering, San Francisco, 13-15 October, 1976, 164-168.

24. Elshoff, J.L. "An Analysis of Some Commercial PL/1 Programs". IEEE Transactions on Software Engineering. SE-Z, 1976, 113-120.

25. Fink, R.C. "Major Issues Involving the Development of an Effective Management Control System for Software Maintenance". Proceedings, COMPSAC 77, Chicago, November 8-11, 1977, 533-538.

26. Fisher, D.A. "DoD's Common Programming Language Effort". Computer, March 1978, 25-33.

27. Gildersleeve, T.R. Data Processing Project Management, New York: Van Nostrand Reinhold, 1974.

28. Gundermann, R.E. "A Glimpse Into Program Maintenance". Datamation 19, June 1973, 99-101.

29. "Implications of Using Modular Programming". Guide No. 1, Hoskyns Systems Research, London, 1973.

30. Jones, R.A. "Maintenance Considered Harmful". ACM Forum. Communications of the ACM 21, 1978, 882.

31. Khan, Z. "How to Tackle the Systems Maintenance Dilemma". Canadian Data Systems, March 1975, 30-32.

32. Knudsen, D.B., A. Barofsky, and L.R. Satz. "A Modification Request Control System". Proceedings, 2nd International Conference on Software Engineering, San Francisco, 13-15 October, 1976, 187-190.

33. Kosy, D. "Air Force Command and Control Information Processing in the 1980's". U.S. Air Force Project RAND, Rand Corporation, June 1971.

34. Lientz, B.P. and M. Chen. "A Methodology for Long Range Information Services Planning". Long Range Planning, September, 1979.

35. Lientz, B.P. and E.B. Swanson. "Discovering Issues in Application Software Maintenance". Data Management, 16, September 1978.

36. Lientz, B.P. and E.B. Swanson. "Problem Factors and Determinants in Application Software Maintenance". Information Systems Working Paper 7-79, Graduate School of Management, University of California, Los Angeles, March 1979.

37. Lientz, B.P. and E.B. Swanson. "Software Maintenance: A User/Management Tug-of-War". Data Management, 17, April 1979, 26-30.

38. Lientz, B.P. and E.B. Swanson. "The Impact of Development Productivity Aids on Application Software Maintenance". Proceedings, Conference on Application Development Systems, San Jose, California, March 9-11, 1980.

39. Lientz, B.P., E.B. Swanson, and G.E. Tompkins. "Characteristics of Application Software Maintenance". Communications of the ACM 21, 1978, 466-471.

40. Lindhorst, W.M. "Scheduled Maintenance of Applications Software". Datamation 19, May 1973, 87-89.

41. Liu, C.C. "A Look at Software Maintenance". *Datamation*, 22, November 1976, 51-55.

42. Mason, R.O. and E.B. Swanson. "Measurement for Management Decision: A Perspective". *California Management Review*, 21, Spring 1979, 70-81.

43. McLean, E.R. "End Users as Application Developers". Paper to be presented at the Application Development Symposium sponsored by GUIDE/SHARE/IBM, Monterey, California, October 14-17, 1979.

44. Merwin, R.E. "Guest Editorial: Software Management: We Must Find a Way". *IEEE Transactions on Software Engineering*, SE-4, July 1978, 307-308.

45. Mills, H.D. "Software Development". *IEEE Transactions on Software Engineering*, SE-2, December 1976, 265-273.

46. Mooney, J.W. "Organization Program Maintenance". *Datamation* 21, February 1975, 63-66.

47. Nie, N.H. et al *SPSS*. 2nd Edition. New York: McGraw-Hill, 1975.

48. Nolan, R.L. "Managing the Computer Resource: A Stage Hypothesis," *Communications of the ACM* 16, 1973, 399-405.

49. Ogdin, J.L. "Designing Reliable Software". *Datamation*, 18, July 1972, 71- 78.

50. Perry, W.E. and J. FitzGerald. "Designing for Auditability". *Datamation*, 23, August 1977, 46-50.

51. "Program Maintenance: User's View". *Data Processing* 7, 1973, 1-4.

52. Punter, M. "Programming for Maintenance". *Data Processing*, September-October 1975, 292-294.

53. Riggs, R. "Computer System Maintenance". Datamation 15, November 1969, 227-235.

54. Rose, L.A. Letter to the Editor. Datamation, 24, December 1978, 42.

55. Sackman, H. Computers, System Science, and Evolving Society. New York: Wiley, 1967.

56. Sharpley, W.K., Jr. "Software Maintenance Planning for Embedded Computer Systems". Proceedings, COMPSAC 77, Chicago, November 8-11, 1977, 520-526.

57. Sterns, S. "Experience with Centralyzed Maintenance of a Large Application System". IEEE Computer Society Proceedings 45, 1975, 297-302.

58. Swanson, E.B. "On the User-Requisite Variety of Computer Application Software". IEEE Transactions on Reliability. R-28, August 1979, 221-226.

59. Swanson, E.B. "The Dimensions of Maintenance". Proceedings, 2nd International Conference on Software Engineering, San Francisco, 13-15 October, 1976, 492-497.

60. Swanson, E.B. "The 'Sub O' Approach to Information System Development". Proceedings, Hawaii International Conference on System Sciences, Honolulu, January 4-5, 1979, 122-131.

61. Taggart, W.M., Jr. and Tharp, M.O. "A Survey of Information Requirements Analysis Techniques". ACM Computing Surveys, 9, December 1977, 273-290.

62. Teichroew, D. and E.A. Hershey, III. "PSL/PSA: A Computer-Aided Technique for Structured Documentation and Analysis of Information Processing Systems". IEEE Transactions on Software Engineering, SE- 3, January 1977, 41-48.

63. Tompkins, G.E. "Characteristics of the High Cost of Maintenance". Unpublished Ph.D dissertation, Graduate School of Management, University of California, Los Angeles, 1977.

64. Winograd, T. "Beyond Programming Languages". Communications of the ACM, 22, July 1979, 391-401.

65. Yourdon, E. Techniques of Program Structure and Design. Englewood Cliffs, N.J.: Prentice-Hall, 1975.

66. Zloof, M.M. "Query-by-Example: A Data Base Language". IBM Systems Journal, 16, 1977, 324-343.

APPENDIX

I Questionnaire

The questionnaire used in the research is reprinted in unaltered form on the following pages.

A QUESTIONNAIRE

ON

APPLICATION SOFTWARE MAINTENANCE

The Information Studies Center
Graduate School of Management
University of California
Los Angeles
Los Angeles, California 90024

INTRODUCTION

The purpose of the questionnaire is to assess some characteristics of application software maintenance, as it is performed within Data Processing organizations of various types and sizes. As used here, the term "maintenance" refers to all modifications made to an existing application system, including enhancements and extensions.

The questionnaire consists of two parts. The first contains questions on the Data Processing Department. The second, questions on a particular application system maintained by the Department.

The questionnaire should be completed by the manager of the Data Processing Department, with the assistance of his or her staff.

Some of the questions call for facts which may or may not be readily determined, given the data available. These questions are accompanied by the following, permitting you to indicate the basis of your answer:

```
-------------------------------------------------
 Check the applicable statement:

 The above answer is:
 Reasonably accurate, based on good data _____
 A rough estimate, based on minimal data _____
 A  best  guess, not based  on  any data _____
-------------------------------------------------
```

Please answer each question, even where you must guess in the absence of data.

Space for "remarks" is also frequently included. Where you feel that your answer can be usefully clarified, please enter your remarks accordingly.

Your assistance and cooperation is greatly appreciated. To ensure complete confidentiality, the questionnaire has been designed so that the organizations responding may remain anonymous.

PART I

The Data Processing Department

1.1 To what industry does the organization served by the Data Processing Department belong? (Check the one which most closely applies.)

Manufacturing industries:

a.	Data Processing Equipment	|_____|
b.	Instruments/Electrical	|_____|
c.	Chemical/Allied Products	|_____|
d.	Printing/Publishing	|_____|
e.	Food/Tobacco	|_____|
f.	Primary/Fabricated Metal	|_____|
g.	Transportation Equipment	|_____|
h.	Petroleum/Coal/Rubber	|_____|
i.	Paper/Paper Products	|_____|
j.	Textiles/Apparel	|_____|
k.	Other (Please indicate) _____	

Non-manufacturing industries:

l.	Insurance	|_____|
m.	Banking/Credit Agency	|_____|
n.	EDP Services	|_____|
o.	Education	|_____|
p.	Government	|_____|
q.	Public Utility	|_____|
r.	Investment	|_____|
s.	Mining/Construction	|_____|
t.	Transportation	|_____|
u.	Consultants	|_____|
v.	Other (Please indicate) _____	

/7

1.2 What is the annual budget of the Data Processing Department for data processing equipment rental, maintenance, and amortization expense? (Check the catagory which applies.)

a.	$4,000,000 or more	|_____|	
b.	Less than $4,000,000 but $2,000,000 or more	|_____|	
c.	Less than $2,000,000 but $1,000,000 or more	|_____|	
d.	Less than $1,000,000 but $500,000 or more	|_____|	
e.	Less than $500,000 but $250,000 or more	|_____|	
f.	Less than $250,000 but $125,000 or more	|_____|	
g.	Less than $125,000	|_____|	/9

1.3 What is the total number of equivalent full-time personnel in the Data Processing Department?

|_____| /11-14

Of the total number of equivalent full-time personnel, how many work as applications programmers and/or systems analysts?

|_____| /16-19

1.4 Are those applications programmers and/or systems analysts responsible for the maintenance of existing application systems organized separately from those responsible for new system development?

Yes |_____| No |_____| /21

Remarks:

189

1.5 In terms of the total person-hours worked annually by applications programming and systems analysis personnel, what percentage is currently spent in each of the following activities:

Application system maintenance: _____%

New application system development: _____%

Other: _____%

TOTAL: 100%   /23-28

```
Check the applicable statement:

The above answer is:
Reasonably accurate, based on good data _____
A rough estimate, based on minimal data _____
A best guess, not based on any data _____
```
                                            /30

Two years ago, what were the percentages?

Application system maintenance: _____%

New application system development: _____%

Other: _____%

TOTAL: 100%   /32-37

```
Check the applicable statement:

The above answer is:
Reasonably accurate, based on good data _____
A rough estimate, based on minimal data _____
A best guess, not based on any data _____
```
                                            /39

Remarks:

1.6 As the manager of the Data Processing Department, how demanding on
     your own time are the problems which arise in application system
     maintenance, when compared to those which arise in new application
     system development? (Check one of the following.)

       a. New system development problems by far
           the more demanding |_____|

       b. New system development problems
           somewhat more demanding |_____|

       c. Maintenance and new system development
           problems equally demanding |_____|

       d. Maintenance problems somewhat more
           demanding |_____|

       e. Maintenance problems by far the more
           demanding |_____| /41

Remarks:

1.7 Relative to the tasks at hand, how would you evaluate the current
     level of staffing of the Data Processing Department on the whole?
     (Check one of the following.)

       a. Substantially understaffed: |_____|

       b. Somewhat understaffed: |_____|

       c. Neither understaffed nor overstaffed: |_____|

       d. Somewhat overstaffed: |_____|

       e. Substantially overstaffed: |_____| /43

     Remarks:

191

PART II
The Maintenance of an Application System

2.1 Please identify an application system maintained by the Data Processing Department which: (i) has been operational one year or longer; (ii) represents a significant investment of time and effort by your department; and (iii) is considered by management to be of fundamental importance to the organization.

Name of application system: _____

Basic organizational function (Describe briefly):

/7-8

2.2 On what date (month and year) did the application system become operational?

Month |_____| Year |_____| /10-13

Remarks:

2.3 Is a data base management system employed in the processing of the application system?

Yes |_____| No |_____| /15

If so, which? _____

2.4 What is the total number of programs <u>currently</u> included in the application system maintained? (The term "program" is associated here with a block of source language statements compiled or assembled as a unit.)

|_____| /17-20

<u>Check the applicable statement:</u>

The above answer is:
Reasonably accurate, based on good data _____
A rough estimate, based on minimal data _____
A best guess, not based on any data _____

/22

What was the total number of programs included in the application system <u>one year ago</u>?

|_____| /24-27

<u>Check the applicable statement:</u>

The above answer is:
Reasonably accurate, based on good data _____
A rough estimate, based on minimal data _____
A best guess, not based on any data _____

/29

Remarks:

2.5 What is the total number of source language statements (excluding comments) <u>currently</u> included in the application system maintained?

|_____| /31-35

```
-------------------------------------------------
Check the applicable statement:

The above answer is:
Reasonably accurate, based on good data _____
A rough estimate, based on minimal data _____
A best guess,  not  based  on  any data _____
-------------------------------------------------
```
/37

What was the total number of source language statements (excluding comments) included in the application system <u>one year ago</u>?

|_____| /39-43

```
-------------------------------------------------
Check the applicable statement:

The above answer is:
Reasonably accurate, based on good data _____
A rough estimate, based on minimal data _____
A best guess,  not  based  on any  data _____
-------------------------------------------------
```
/45

Remarks:

2.6 Of the total number of source language statements currently
maintained, what percentage is written in each of the following
languages?

COBOL	|____|%	
Assembler	|____|%	
PL/1	|____|%	
RPG	|____|%	
FORTRAN	|____|%	
Others (Please indicate):		
_____	|____|%	
_____	|____|%	
TOTAL:	100%	/47-60

```
Check the applicable statement:

The above answer is:
Reasonably accurate, based on good data  _____
A rough estimate, based on minimal data  _____
A best guess,  not  based  on  any data  _____
```
/62

Remarks:

2.7 How many individual data files currently make up the data base
     associated with the application system? (The term "data base"
     is defined here simply as the set of master files associated with
     the system.)

                                                    |_____| /7-9

     Remarks:

2.8 What is the <u>current</u> size of the data base, measured in total number
     of bytes (or the equivalent)?

                                                    |_____| /11-16

     ```
     ------------------------------------------------
     | Check the applicable statement:              |
     |                                              |
     | The above answer is:                         |
     | Reasonably accurate, based on good data _____|
     | A rough estimate, based on minimal data _____|
     | A best  guess,  not  based  on  any data _____|    /18
     ------------------------------------------------
     ```

     What was the size of the data base, measured in total number of
     bytes (or the equivalent) <u>one year ago</u>?

                                                    |_____| /20-25

     ```
     ------------------------------------------------
     | Check the applicable statement:              |
     |                                              |
     | The above answer is:                         |
     | Reasonably accurate, based on good data _____|
     | A rough estimate, based on minimal data _____|
     | A best  guess,  not  based  on  any data _____|    /27
     ------------------------------------------------
     ```

     Remarks:

2.9 How many pre-defined user reports are <u>currently</u> associated with the application system maintained?

|_____| /29-32

```
------------------------------------------------
| Check the applicable statement:                |
|                                                |
| The above answer is:                           |
| Reasonably accurate, based on good data  _____ |
| A rough estimate, based on minimal data  _____ |
| A best guess,  not  based  on  any data  _____ |     /34
------------------------------------------------
```

How many pre-defined user reports were associated with the application system <u>one year ago</u>?

|_____| /36-39

```
------------------------------------------------
| Check the applicable statement:                |
|                                                |
| The above answer is:                           |
| Reasonably accurate, based on good data  _____ |
| A rough estimate, based on minimal data  _____ |
| A best guess,  not  based  on  any data  _____ |     /41
------------------------------------------------
```

Remarks:

2.10 Which of the following tools, methods and techniques were employed
in the development of the application system maintained? (Check all
those which apply.)

    a.   Decision tables |____|

    b.   Data base dictionary |____|

    c.   Test data generators |____|

    d.   Structured programming |____|

    e.   Automated flowcharting |____|

    f.   HIPO (Hierarchy plus Input-Process-Output)
       Design Aid Technique |____|

    g.   Structured Walk-Through |____|

    h.   Chief Programmer Team |____|

        Others (Please indicate):

    i. _____ |____|

    j. _____ |____|

    k. _____ |____| /43-53

2.11 What is the total number of person-hours now expended annually on
maintenance of the application system?

                                        |_____| /55-60

```
---------------------------------------------------
| Check the applicable statement:                 |
|                                                 |
| The above answer is:                            |
| Reasonably accurate, based on good data _____   |
| A rough estimate, based on minimal data _____   |
| A best guess, not based on any data _____       |
---------------------------------------------------
```
    /62

Remarks:

2.12 Of the total number of person-hours now expended annually on
maintenance of the application system, what percentage is expended
in each of the following problem areas:

a.   Emergency program fixes |_____|%

b.   Routine debugging |_____|%

c.   Accommodation of changes to data
       inputs and files |_____|%

d.   Accommodation of changes to hardware
       and system software |_____|%

e.   Enhancements for users |_____|%

f.   Improvement of program documentation |_____|%

g.   Recoding for efficiency in computation |_____|%

Others (Please indicate):

h.   _____ |_____|%

i.   _____ |_____|%

                              TOTAL: 100%   /7-24

```
Check the applicable statement:

The above answer is:
Reasonably accurate, based on good data _____
A rough estimate, based on minimal data _____
A best guess, not based on any data _____
```
           /26

Remarks:

2.13 Of the total number of person-hours now expended annually on providing enhancements for users in maintenance of the application system, what percentage is expended in each of the following problem areas:

a. Providing new, additional reports _____%

b. Adding data to existing reports _____%

c. Reformating existing reports, without changing their data content _____%

d. Condensation of data in existing reports _____%

e. Consolidation of existing reports, reducing the number of reports _____%

Others (please indicate):

f. _____ _____%

g. _____ _____%

TOTAL 100% /28-41

Check the applicable statement:

The above answer is:
Reasonably accurate, based on good data _____
A rough estimate, based on minimal data _____
A best guess, not based on any data _____

/43

Remarks:

2.14 What is the total number of individuals currently assigned (in whole or in part) to maintenance of the application system?

|_____| /45-46

Of the total number of individuals currently assigned, how many worked previously on the <u>development</u> of this same application system?

|_____| /48-49

2.15 What organizational controls are established for the maintenance of the application system? (Check all those which apply.)

    a.   All user requests for changes to the application system must be logged and documented |_____|

    b.   All user requests for changes to the application system must be cost justified |_____|

    c.   All troubles encountered in the operational processing of the application system programs must be logged and documented |_____|

    d.   All changes to the application programs must be logged and documented |_____|

    e.   All changes to the application programs must undergo a formal retest procedure |_____|

    f.   With the exception of emergency fixes, all changes to the application programs are batched for periodic implementation according to a predetermined schedule |_____|

    g.   A formal audit of the application system is made periodically |_____|

    h.   Equipment costs associated with operating and maintaining the application system are charged back (in whole or in part) to the user |_____|

    i.   Personnel costs associated with operating and maintaining the application system are charged back (in whole or in part) to the user |_____| /51-59

2.16 In your judgment, to what extent are (or have been) the following a problem in maintaining the application system? (Check the appropriate category.)

		No Problem At All				
			Somewhat Minor Problem			
				Minor Problem		
					Somewhat Major Problem	
						Major Problem
		5	4	3	2	1
a.	Turnover of maintenance personnel					
b.	Quality of application system documentation					
c.	Changes made to system hardware and software					
d.	User demand for enhancements and extensions to application system					
e.	Skills of maintenance programming personnel					
f.	Quality of original programming of application system					
g.	Number of maintenance programming personnel available					
h.	Competing demands for maintenance programming personnel time					
i.	Lack of user interest in application system					
j.	Application system run failures					
k.	Lack of user understanding of application system					

/7-17

(continued next page)

	Major Problem	Somewhat Major Problem	Minor Problem	Somewhat Minor Problem	No Problem At All
	5	4	3	2	1
l. Storage requirements of application system programs					
m. Processing time requirements of application system programs					
n. Motivation of maintenance programming personnel					
o. Forecasting of maintenance programming personnel requirements					
p. Maintenance programming productivity					
q. System hardware and software reliability					
r. Data integrity in application system					
s. Unrealistic user expectations					
t. Adherence to programming standards in maintenance					
u. Management support of application system					
v. Adequacy of application system design specifications					
w. Budgetary pressures					
x. Meeting scheduled commitments					

/18-30

(continued next page)

	Major Problem	Somewhat Major Problem	Minor Problem	Somewhat Minor Problem	No Problem At All
	5	4	3	2	1
y. Inadequate training of user personnel					
z. Turnover in user organization					
Others (Please indicate)					
_____					
_____					

/31-34

-END OF QUESTIONNAIRE-

Thank you for your cooperation!

Please place the completed questionnaire in the envelope provided and mail it back to us.

APPENDIX
II Data Analysis

The purpose of this appendix is to discuss briefly the approach to the analysis of the questionnaire data.

The first part of the analysis examined the response distributions associated with each item of the questionnaire. The results of this analysis are contained in the "Basic Descriptive Results" sections of Chapters 3-7. One consequence of this analysis was the decision to use logarithmic transformations of the measures of application system size and magnitude of maintenance effort in the parametric analysis to follow. (See Chapters 4 and 5.)

A major purpose of the survey was to provide the data processing community with a representative description of application software maintenance, as it currently exists. Hence the descriptive results were held to be important in their own right, not only as background for the analysis of relationships.

The analyses of relationships among the data were largely exploratory. While various hypotheses were suggested from the preliminary study of the literature (see Chapter 1), the survey was not designed as an exercise in the testing of a few well-defined hypotheses. This was considered premature, in an area where little theory exists, within which to incorporate such results. Instead, it was the overall _pattern_ of relationships among the data that was of principal interest.

Establishing the pattern of relationships in a study such as this is a non-trivial task. Due to complexity and diversity within the population studied, it was expected that statistical relationships among the data, e.g. as reflected by correlation coefficients, would provide weak signals of the underlying causal structures. In other words, measures of association were expected to be slight in magnitude. On the other hand, the size of the sample insured that a substantial number of these associations would be found to be statistically significant. There would thus be many of these weak signals.

To establish a provisional filter on this signalling process, correlation coefficients were held to be "notable" only if they were of absolute magnitude 0.100 or greater. The setting of the filter at this level of discrimination was not based on an _a priori_ logic; rather it was tailored to the specific results at hand, to yield a number of relationships both sufficiently rich and sufficiently manageable.

Analyses of relationships were carried out by means of correlation and contingency table analyses, analyses of variance, and regression analyses. Factor analysis was also employed, to ascertain the dimensions associated with the problems in maintenance. The techniques are well described from a user's point of view in Nie, et. al. (1975).

The search for a pattern among the relationships may be likened to the completion of a jigsaw puzzle. Certain pieces obviously go together; others do not. The trick is to fit all the pieces together to make an overall sense, an intelligible picture. In the case of the jigsaw puzzle, there is one solution to this problem. Alas, in the case of our exploratory research, there may be several such "solutions." Further, certain pieces to the puzzle are likely to be missing.

Nevertheless, many more pictures of the maintenance process will be inconsistent with the full pattern of results, than will be consistent. The solution space is thus substantially narrowed. Further, our own suggested "solution" to the puzzle, the picture we have perceived, may now be validated by other researchers, working with other tools of observation and inference. In this way, progress toward a theory of software maintenance may be made.

INDEX

A

accounts receivable - 34
adaptive maintenance - 68, 105
adequacy of data on size - 54
age and controls - 103
age and system size - 59
age of applications - 38ff
allocation of effort - 68, 71
allocation of effort and tools - 109
analysts/programmers - 23
analyst workbench - 163
APL - 176
applications in survey - 33
Assembler - 47
audit - 98, 101
automated flowcharting - 36, 56

B

Bariff, M. - 164
batching of changes - 98, 101

maintenance escort - 174
maintenance time - 18
management of time - 16
management support - 122
Mashey, R. - 161
Merwin, E. - 158
Mills, H. - 155
modular design - 7
Mooney, J. - 4, 154
motivation of personnel - 8

N

Nie, N. - 125
Nolan, R. - 31, 164, 169
normal distribution - 42
number of programs - 34, 42
number of programs and predefined user reports - 57
number of source statements - 35, 42
Nyman, R. - 176

O

office systems - 176
Oglin, J. - 4, 6
older vs. younger systems - 35
on-line change - 7
operations trouble log - 105
order entry - 34
organizational design experiments - 162
organizational issues - 6, 154
organization and staffing adequacy - 31
organization categories in survey - 17, 20
organization controls - 98ff
organization size and controls - 111
Osajima, H. - 6

P

payroll - 34
perfective maintenance - 68, 107
personnel charge-back - 98, 101
personnel turnover - 8
PL/I - 35, 47
portfolio management - 158
pre-defined user reports - 34, 42, 51, 52
preliminary survey - 9ff
principal language in application - 53
problem area issue - 8
problems in maintenance - 9
problems of maintenance - 115ff
processing time requirements - 122
production programming - 8
productivity technique issues - 7, 155

product quality - 116
product quality and tools - 118
program growth and productivity aids - 36
programmer effectiveness - 116
programmer time availability - 116
program size - 34
Punter, M. - 8

Q, R

Query by Example - 161
questionnaire - 11ff, 185ff
recoding for efficiency - 68, 73
reliability and data base dictionary - 142
reliability of hardware/software - 122
report consolidation - 68, 74
retest procedure - 98
Riggs, R. - 4, 8
Rose, R. - 142
routine debugging - 73
RPG - 35, 47
run failures - 122

S

Salisbury, W. - 167
scale of effort issues - 5, 153
separate organization of maintenance - 16, 30
skills of maintenance staff - 121
software management - 158
software update - 5
Spaniol, R. - 11
SPSS statistical package - 13
staffing and previous experience - 75
staffing levels - 16, 18
standards - 122
Stanley, R. - 163
storage requirements - 122
structured programming - 35, 56
structured programming and user knowledge - 139
structured walk-through - 35, 56
survey administration - 11ff
survey design - 11
Swanson, B. - 4, 10, 68, 103, 107
system reliability - 116
system size and routine debugging - 82
system size measures - correlation - 58

T

Taggart, W. - 160
technical vs. nontechnical problems - 124
Teichroew, D. - 160
test data generators - 7, 35, 56

Tharp, M. - 160
Tompkins, G. - 9
tools and problem factors - 139
training - 124
turnover of personnel - 121

U, V

unitary maintenance organization - 173
user based performance specifications - 170
user demands - 9
user enhancements - 68, 121
user knowledge - 116
user organization turnover - 123
user problem studies - 160

W, X, Y, Z

Winogard, T. - 152
Yourdon, E. - 5
Zloof, M. - 161

DATE DUE

DEMCO NO. 38-298